KREGEL CLASSIC

CLASSIC SERMONS ON THE PARABLES OF JESUS

Compiled by
Warren W. Wiersbe

kregel
PUBLICATIONS

Grand Rapids, MI 49501

Classic Sermons on the Parables of Jesus
Compiled by Warren W. Wiersbe

Published by Kregel Publications, a division of Kregel, Inc.,
P.O. Box 2607, Grand Rapids, MI 49501. Kregel Publications provides trusted, biblical publications for Christian
growth and service. Your comments and suggestions are
valued.

Cover photo: © 1996, COMSTOCK INC.
Cover and book design: Alan G. Hartman

Library of Congress Cataloging-in-Publication Data

Classic sermons on the parables of Jesus / [compiled
by] Warren W. Wiersbe.
    p.   cm.— (Kregel classic sermons series)
  Includes index.
    1. Jesus Christ—Parables—Sermons. 2. Sermons,
American. 3. Sermons, English. I. Wiersbe, Warren W.
II. Series
BT375.2.C57   1997   252—dc21   96-45062
                                               CIP

ISBN   0-8254-4078-5

Printed in the United States of America
2 3 4 5 / 01 00

CONTENTS

LIST OF SCRIPTURE TEXTS

PREFACE

THE *KREGEL CLASSIC SERMONS SERIES* is an attempt to assemble and publish meaningful sermons from master preachers about significant themes. These are *sermons,* not essays or chapters taken from books about themes. Not all of these sermons could be called great, but all of them are *meaningful.* They apply the truths of the Bible to the needs of the human heart, which is something that all effective preaching must do.

While some are better known than others, all of the preachers whose sermons I have selected had important ministries and were highly respected in their day. The fact that a sermon is included in this volume does not mean that either the compiler or the publisher agrees with or endorses everything that the man did, preached, or wrote. The sermon is here because it has a valued contribution to make.

These are sermons about *significant* themes. The pulpit is no place to play with trivia. The preacher has thirty minutes in which to help mend broken hearts, change defeated lives, and save lost souls; he can never accomplish this demanding ministry by distributing homiletical tidbits. In these difficult days we do not need clever pulpiteers who discuss the times; we need dedicated ambassadors who will preach the eternities.

The reading of these sermons can enrich your spiritual life. The studying of them can enrich your skills as an interpreter and expounder of God's truth. However God uses these sermons in your life and ministry, my prayer is that His church around the world will be encouraged and strengthened by them.

WARREN W. WIERSBE

A Soul to Let

George H. Morrison (1866–1928) assisted the great Alexander Whyte in Edinburgh, pastored two churches, and then became pastor in 1902 of the distinguished Wellington Church on University Avenue in Glasgow, Scotland. His preaching drew great crowds; in fact, people had to line up an hour before the services to be sure to get seats in the large auditorium. Morrison was a master of imagination in preaching, yet his messages are solidly biblical.

From his many published volumes of sermons, I have chosen this message, found in *Sunrise*, published in 1903 by Hodder and Stoughton, London.

George H. Morrison

1

A SOUL TO LET

Matthew 12:43–44

OUR LORD HAD a quick eye for moral tragedies, and in the pictorial setting of these two verses He has delineated one of the saddest of them all. One marvels at the sure touch of Christ in dealing with the disasters of the soul. Men felt instinctively that He would understand them, and so they came to Him when things were going wrong. And one of the inexplicable wonders about Jesus is this sure insight into secret failures. When we have failed, we grasp a brother's failure, our insight is the child of fellow-feeling. There are whole ranks of tragedies we never suspect just because God has mercifully guarded us from them. But Christ, in the panoply of perfect manhood, was separated from every taint of sin, and yet had an exquisite understanding of the sinner. It is something, my brother, to feel that you are known. Your tragedy is not so secret as you thought. You are haunted with a dull sense tonight that unless there is effort and clearing of your feet, your last state is going to be worse than your first. Christ has spoken on that theme long ago.

Now what strikes us first in this man with an unclean spirit is that all his tragedy was underground. I mean by that that his very nearest and dearest never suspected what had been going on. If you had asked some villager about him, he would have answered, "He is an unclean beast." And if ten years later you had asked again, you would have been told he had been going down hill steadily. Steadily, gradually, so it had seemed to everybody. Always a little worse, a little lower. And only Christ knew that that view was false—

the man had been standing at the gates of freedom once! He had played the man against his tyrannous vices. He had cast them out, and . . . cried to God to help him. He had breathed . . . liberty, and tasted the joy of triumph, and known what a noble thing it was to live! And when the ousted tenants came back again, and the old disorder began to reign within, none knew but Christ the struggle, the cry, the passion to be free, of the man whom all the village thought a prisoner.

Are not many of our tragedies underground? They are transacted in the hidden sphere. There are molten fires under the vines of Etna. There are hidden graves among the garden flowers. And we sow and water the flowers in our garden just to conceal the sepulcher that is there. Who knows how you have dreamed, how you have struggled? And men look at you and call you contented, merry! But there are memories of prayer stored in your heart and of days when your life seemed utterly unworthy, and you stood up and cast the devils out. And they are all back again tonight, and never a soul in this city knows of it, except yourself and Christ.

But there is another feature in this story besides its secrecy. It is the story of an unused triumph. This man did not fail because he never won; there was one morning when his heart was clean. That was his day of victory, and the promise of final conquest was in that, but he misused his victory and was lost. One of the saddest stories ever written is just the story of our mismanaged triumphs. It is our little victories that curse us because we have neither head nor heart to manage them. We are so apt to be self-centered in success; so ready to forget how weak we are; so prone to think that the campaign is ours because in one skirmish the enemy has fled. Then we grow careless, we do not walk with God; we do not garrison our heart against assault. In an hour when we think not comes the old temptation, strong, subtle, doubly sweet because foresworn, and we are taken unawares and mastered. Our last state is worse than our first.

I have often thought, on reading this little parable,

of the wonderful wisdom of Jesus in His victory. I have often thought of the self-restraint of Christ when He triumphed over sin and over death. If there was ever a triumph in the history of earth used for the lasting blessing of mankind, it was the triumph of Jesus when He rose. There was a sweet restraint in resurrection joy. There was no spectacle of a risen Savior for the crowd. There was a watchful reserve, a choosing of times and companies, a holy management of the resurrection glory that marks the risen Savior as divine. Even Christ was guarded in His hour of triumph—how much more guarded should the Christian be? This man cast out the unclean spirit and said all is well. And his last state was worse than his first!

And you see what his peculiar danger was? It was the peril of the empty heart. His soul lay vacant, that was the pity of it. There was room for the ousted Devil to return. Some men are tempted because their hearts are full. Life is so rich, so strong in a thousand interests, there is no room in it for Christ at all. But many are tempted because their hearts are empty, and the old ways creep back again to stay. It is not sufficient to expel the wrong. We must fill the emptied heart with nobler things. A tenantless heart—a soul that is to let—is a standing invitation to the Devil.

It was there the man of our story failed. Have you never failed just at that point? There was struggle with evil and momentary triumph, there was an empty and swept and garnished house. And that was something; you were right proud of it, after the moral disorder of the past. But you forgot that a habit expelled is not by any means a habit slain. You forgot that new interests must fill the life if the old interests are never to lodge again. It was because no ruling passion had been begotten that you began to hanker for the old again. It was because there was no new enthusiasm, no worthier tenants to occupy the soul, that you craved for the ousted things and drew them back. Had the empty house been filled with a new purpose, controlled by a new hand and nobler will, the cast-out spirit would have acknowledged defeat and felt there was no room in that soul for him. It was the soul to let that did the harm.

And so I bring you face to face with the great mystery of an indwelling Christ. I want you to set that truth in the light of all I have been saying until you see how practical it is. These deepest doctrines of the Word of God were never meant to be speculative wonders—it is when we live them we find how real they are—and it is Christ in you, the hope of glory, that saves you from the peril of the empty heart. The Gospel does not merely come to you and say, "My brother, my sister, you must give up that sin." It does not bid you empty your heart of evil, and leave it empty and garnished to the end. It knows the danger of a soul unoccupied; the certain fall of a heart without a tenant. And so the Gospel is prepared to give you something far better than what it drives away. It is prepared to inhabit the temple of your heart with the Holy Spirit of the Lord Jesus Christ. Do you not know that your bodies are temples of the Holy Spirit who dwells in you? That is the glad exchange the Gospel makes. In place of the unclean spirit who is gone, the Spirit of the Lord comes in to dwell.

Now where the Spirit of the Lord is, there is liberty, and where the Spirit of the Lord is, there is life. And it is that new liberty and life within the heart that make us strong when old things steal back again. "I can do all things," cried the apostle—not through a barred door and an empty heart—"I can do all things through Christ which strengtheneth me"; his empty and swept and garnished heart was full. O brother, you have been fighting out your sin. But what you want is a new enthusiasm in its place. I wish to ask you seriously and simply, have you ever made room for Him to take Him in? There is love, there is power, there is liberty in Christ. Open your heart. Receive the gift of God. It is in the bitter hour of temptation that men find the worth of an indwelling Savior.

For our old sins are hungering to get back. That

truth is clearly written in our text. They are houseless and homeless, and restless and ill at ease. They crave their old shelter in our lives again. And you do not mean to give it to them. No! You are done with the past forever and a day. But so was the hero of our text tonight, and yet his last state was to be lost. Your castoff vices are not dead. They are going to return in subtle ways. Do not pride yourself on a swept and garnished house; there is no pledge of victory in that. But there *is* in a heart where dwells the love of Christ, and something of the high power of His passion. It is in Him that we are more than conquerors. It is in Him that our last state shall be our best.

> Oh! come to my heart, Lord Jesus,
> There is room in my heart for Thee.

The Sinner's Excuses Swept Away

Dwight Lyman Moody (1837–1899) is known around the world as one of America's most effective evangelists. Converted as a teenager through the witness of his Sunday school teacher, Moody became active in YMCA and Sunday school work in Chicago while pursuing a successful business career. He then devoted his full time to evangelism and was used mightily of God in campaigns in both the United States and Great Britain. He founded the Northfield School for girls, the Mount Hermon School for boys, the Northfield Bible Conference, and the Moody Bible Institute in Chicago. Before the days of planes and radio, Moody traveled more than a million miles and addressed more than one hundred million people.

This message is taken from *The Best of D. L. Moody*, edited by Wilbur M. Smith and published in 1971 by Moody Press.

Dwight Lyman Moody

2

THE SINNER'S EXCUSES SWEPT AWAY

Luke 14:15–24

CHRIST HAD BEEN invited to dine with a rich Pharisee. It seemed as though this man had gathered his friends together in a kind of conspiracy to catch Christ. They watched Him. A man who had had dropsy was placed before Jesus, as though they wanted to see what He would do. Christ read their hearts, and so before He healed the man He asked them if it was lawful to heal on the Sabbath day. But they didn't want to answer, for fear they'd betray themselves, and so they held their peace. Then Christ put the question to them in another way. He asked them if any of them had an ox or an ass fall into a pit, should he not straightway pull him out on the Sabbath day. Then he healed the man, as the Pharisees and lawyers weren't able to answer Him.

Then he told them about the feast and told them to be humble. When a man prepares a feast, men rush in; but when God prepares one they all begin to make excuses and don't want to go. The first excuse was that made by Adam, "The woman thou gavest me, she gave me to eat." These men that excused themselves made manufactured excuses; they didn't really have any. The drunkard, the libertine, the businessman, the citizen, the harlot, all had their excuses. If God were to take men at their word about these excuses, and swept every one into his grave who had an excuse, there would be a very small congregation in the Tabernacle next Sunday, there would be little business in Chicago, and in a few weeks the grass would be growing on these busy streets. Every man who was nursing a sin had an excuse, as though God had asked them to go into a plague-stricken city, or a hospital, or to hear a dry lecture, or something repelling and objectionable, something that wasn't for their greatest good.

Take the excuses. There wasn't one that wasn't a lie. The Devil made them all. If the sinner hadn't one already, the Devil was there at his elbow to suggest one about the truth of the Bible or something of that sort. One of the excuses mentioned was that the man invited had bought a piece of ground and had to look at it. Real estate and corner lots were keeping a good many men out of God's kingdom. It was a lie to say that he had to go and see it then, for he ought to have looked at it before he bought it. Then the next man said he'd bought some oxen and must prove them. That was another lie. If he hadn't proved them before he bought them, he ought to have and could have done it after the supper just as well as before it. But the third man had the silliest, the worst excuse of all. He said he had married a wife and couldn't come. Why didn't he bring her with him? She would have liked the supper just as well as he and would have enjoyed a supper, as almost any young bride would.

These seemed to be foolish excuses, but they were not any more so than the excuses of today. Indeed, the excuses of men are getting worse and worse all the time. They say they can't believe the Bible; it's so mysterious. Well, what of it? Infidels, skeptics, pantheists, deists said they didn't believe the Bible. Had they ever used it? Did they read it as carefully as they read any other book? This was their excuse. If everybody could understand everything the Bible said, it wouldn't be God's book. If Christians, if theologians had studied it for forty, fifty, sixty years, and then only began to understand it, how could a man expect to understand it by one reading? A child the first day at school couldn't even know the alphabet, and yet it wasn't a sign that it was a poor school because he didn't learn the first day all about grammar, arithmetic, and geometry.

Another said God was a hard Master. No; that was

one of Satan's lies. The Devil is the hard master. In the Tombs in New York there is over the door the remark, "The way of the transgressor is hard." God's yoke is easy, His burden light. Ask prisoners, ask gamblers, ask sinners, if Satan's yoke is easy. It's the hardest of all. God's service a hard one! How will that sound in the judgment? Many said it wasn't that, but there is such a struggle. Wasn't all life a struggle? Some said they were wicked. Those are just the kind Jesus came to save. They weren't too wicked to be saved. They were so worldly minded, so hard-hearted, that was another falsehood. Look at what God did for Bunyan and John Newton and many others who were the wickedest, and even the thief on the cross. God is already reconciled; He doesn't need the sinner to be reconciled to Him. The Lord prepares the sinner.

Yet you hear people say they can't understand that; they cannot imagine but *they* have to do something to satisfy God. But I tell you that God is satisfied, God is reconciled. You have the word of Paul that God is reconciled to us. Yes, thank God, He is reconciled to the world. Can *you* reconcile God? Christ has done that. The moment a sinner takes this to heart and comes to Jesus, that moment he is saved. Perhaps a story will illustrate this as well as anything.

In England I was told about an only son—these only sons are hard to bring up properly. They have every whim and caprice gratified. They generally grow up headstrong, self-willed, and obstinate, and make it miserable for anyone to have anything to do with them. Well, this son had a father something like himself in disposition. One day a quarrel arose between them, and at last, as the son would not give in and own he was wrong, the father, in a fit of anger, said that he wished his son would leave his house and never come back again. "Well," rejoined the boy (as angry as his father), "I will leave, and I never will enter your house again until you ask me." "Well, then, you won't come back in a hurry," replied his father. The boy then left. The father gave up the boy, but the mother did not.

Perhaps these men here won't understand that, but you women do.

A great many things will separate a man from his wife, a father from his son, but nothing in the wide, wide world will ever separate a mother from her child. A jury can bring in a verdict against her son; the hisses may go up against him; he is condemned to be hanged; there is not a friendly paper to write an article in his favor. But if his mother be there, the boy has at least one eye to rest upon him, one heart to beat in sympathy with him. He is taken to the cold, damp cell and left to his fate. All forsake him but his mother. She comes there; she puts her arms around his neck; she kisses him; she would spend all the time with him if the officers would allow it. She cannot save him. The day before his execution she sees him for the last time; she has not the courage to see him in the shadow of the gallows. The supreme moment at length arrives; he is led forth, and in a few moments he dangles a corpse. Does the mother then forget him? No; even now she goes to his grave, strews flowers upon it, and waters them with her tears. A mother's love is next to God's love. Death is stronger than everything else; yes, but with the exception of one thing—a mother's love. Death and decay may wreck this city, buildings may cease to exist, everything yields before them but a mother's love.

To refer to the illustration again: When the father had given the boy up, he thought he would never come back. The mother was taken very sick. She had been trying by every means in her power to effect a reconciliation between the father and son. When she found she could not recover from her illness she again renewed her efforts with all the power of a mother's love. She wrote to her son, imploring him to ask his father's forgiveness. He sent word back that he would not write to his father unless his father first wrote to him. "I will never come home until he asks me," he said. The mother began to get lower and lower. Her husband at this time came to the bedside and asked if there was anything he could do for her. "Yes, yes," she cried, "there is one thing—you can send for my boy. That is the only wish I have on earth that is not gratified. If you do not care for him while I am alive, who will care for him when I am gone? I cannot bear to die and leave my child among strangers. Just let me see him and speak to him and I will die in peace." The father said he could not send for him. He could, but he wouldn't. He did not want to. The mother has but a few hours now to live. She again beseeches her husband that he will send for their son. The father said he would send a dispatch to him, but in her name. "No, no; that would not do." Well, he can stand it no longer, and he signs his own name at the foot of the telegram. It was sent, and the moment the boy received it he took the first train home.

The father was standing by the side of the bed when the son arrived. But when he saw the door open he turned his back upon him and walked away. The mother grasped the hand of her boy and pressed it again and again, and kissed him fervently. "Oh! Just speak to your father, won't you? Just speak the first word." "No, mother, I will not speak to him until he speaks to me." The excitement was too much and she was rapidly sinking. She told her husband she was dying. She now took his hand in hers, and held the hand of her boy in the other, and sought and strove to bring about a reconciliation. But neither would speak. With her last strength she then placed the hand of the son into the hand of the father and sank down into the arms of death, and was borne by the angels into the kingdom of God. The father looked at the wife and then at the boy; he caught his eye. They fell upon each other's necks, and there stood weeping by the bed of the departed.

That is the illustration I have given, but it is not a fair illustration in this respect: God is not angry with us. With that exception it is a good illustration of reconciliation. Christ brought the hand of the Father clear down to the world; He put the hand of the sinner into the hand of His Father and died that they might be reconciled. You have nothing to do then to bring about a reconciliation. God is already reconciled to us and is ready to save us.

"Blessed is he who shall be at the marriage supper of the Lamb." I have missed a good many appointments in my life, but there is one I will not miss. I would rather be at the marriage feast than have the whole world rolled at my feet. I want to be there and sit down with Isaac and Jacob and Abraham at that supper. It is an invitation for joy and gladness that comes from the King of Kings, from the Lord of glory, to every man and woman in this assembly—the invitation to be at the marriage supper of the Lamb. It is not a personal invitation, but a universal one—"Go out into the highways and hedges and compel them to come in, that my house may be filled." Bid them come, "the poor and the maimed, and the halt, and the blind," to the marriage feast prepared at great expense by our blessed Redeemer.

People began to make excuses very early in the history of Christianity, and they are still at it. Nineteen hundred years have nearly rolled away, and still there are excuses. One of the excuses that we very often hear people giving is that they don't want to become Christians because it will make them gloomy—they will have to put on long faces and button their coats up, cut off all joy and walk through the world until they get to heaven, where they will have pleasure forevermore. We look forward to that happy future, but, thank God, we have some pleasure here. Indeed, no man in the world should be so happy as a man of God. It is one continual source of gladness. He can look up and say, "God is my Father," "Christ is my Savior," and "the church is my mother." All who think otherwise than that a Christian life is one of unceasing joy are deceiving themselves.

I was going by a saloon the other day and saw a sign, "Drink and be merry." Poor, blind, deluded fellows, if they think this will make them merry. If you want to be merry, you must come to the living fountain that bursts from the throne of God; then you will have true pleasure. A man away from God cannot have true pleasure. He is continually thirsting for something he cannot get—thirsting for something that can quench his thirst—he cannot get it until he comes to the living fountain. My friends, that is just another wile of the Devil to keep men from grace. It is false. The more a man is lifted up to heaven, the more joy and peace and gladness he has. He is lifted away from gloom.

Look at a man on his way to execution. Suppose I ran up to him, holding out my hand and saying: "There is a pardon that has been signed by the Governor," and I give it to him. Would he be gloomy and joyless? That is Christ. He comes down with a pardon to us poor men and women on our way to execution. Yonder is a man starving. I go to him and give him bread. Is that going to make him gloomy? A poor man comes along crying with thirst, and I give him a glass of ice water; would that make him gloomy? That's what Christ is doing for us. He has a well of living water, and He asks every thirsty soul to drink freely. Don't you believe for a moment that Christianity is going to make you gloomy.

I remember when I was a boy I thought I would wait until I died and then become a Christian. I thought if I had the consumption, or some lingering disease, I would have plenty of time to become one, and in the meantime I would enjoy the best of the pleasures of the world. My friends, I was at that time under the power of the Devil. The idea that a man has more pleasure away from church is one of the Devil's lies. Do not believe it, but accept this universal invitation to the marriage feast.

I can imagine some men saying, "Mr. Moody has not touched my case at all. That is not the reason why I won't accept Christ. I don't know if I am one of the elect." How often am I met with this excuse—how often do I hear it in the inquiry room! How many men fold their arms and say, "If I am one of the elect I will be saved; and if I ain't, I won't. No use of your bothering

about it." Why don't some of these merchants say, "If
God intends to make me a successful merchant in
Chicago, I will be one whether I like it or not. If He
doesn't, I won't." If you are sick, if a doctor prescribes
for you, don't take the medicine. Throw it out of the
door. It doesn't matter, for if God has decreed you are
going to die, you will; and if He hasn't, you will get
better. If you use that argument you may as well not
walk home from this Tabernacle. If God has said you'll
get home, you'll get there—you'll fly through the air, if
you have been elected to go home. These illustrations
are just the same as the excuse. You cannot go up
there and give that excuse.

The Water of Life is offered freely to everyone. No
unconverted man in the wide, wide world has anything
to do with the doctrine of election any more than I
have to do with the government of China. That epistle
of Paul was written to godly men. Suppose I pick up a
letter and open it, and it tells me about the death of
my wife. Dear me—my wife dead. But I look on the
other side of the letter and find that it is directed to
another man. And so a great many people take Paul's
letter to the churches and take it as a personal letter.
This is what you have to take up: "Whosoever will, let
him drink of the water of life freely." He came down
sixty years after His resurrection and said to John, put
it so broad that no one will mistake it—put it so broad
that no one in Chicago can be stumbling over it—so
that all men may see it plainly—"Whosoever will, let
him drink of the water of life freely."

If you will, you will; if you won't, you won't. Do you
think that God would come down here to give you salvation without giving you the power to take it, and
then condemn you to eternity for not taking it? With
the gift comes the power, and you can take it and live
if you will. Don't stumble over election any more. You
have to deal with that broad proclamation: "Whosoever
will, let him drink of the waters of life freely."

I can imagine someone in the gallery clear up there
saying, "I never have bothered my head about election;

I don't believe men are gloomy when they become Christians. If I was alone I would tell you my reason, but I do not like to get up in this large assemblage and talk here. The fact is, there are hypocrites in the churches. I know a man, a prominent man in the church, who cheated me out of twenty-five dollars. I won't accept this invitation because of those hypocrites in the churches." My friend, you will find very few there if you get to heaven. There won't be a hypocrite in the next world, and if you don't want to be associated with hypocrites in the next world, you will take this invitation. Why, you will find hypocrites everywhere. One of the apostles was himself the very prince of hypocrites, but he didn't get to heaven. You will find plenty of hypocrites in the church. They have been there for the last eighteen hundred years, and will probably remain there. But what is that to you? This is an individual matter between you and your God. Is it because there are hypocrites you are not going to accept the invitation?

"Ah, well, Mr. Moody, that is not my case. I am a businessman, and I have no time. Since the Chicago fire I have had as much as I could attend to in recovering what I lost." If I stood at the door and asked anyone who went out to accept the invitation, I believe hundreds of you would say, "Mr. Moody, you will have to excuse me tonight; time is very precious with me, and you'll have to excuse me." What have you been doing the last twenty, thirty, forty, fifty years that you haven't had a moment to devote to the acceptance of this invitation? That is the cry of the world today: "Time is precious; business must be attended to, and we have no time to spare." Some of you women will say, "I cannot wait; I have to go home and put the children to bed. This is more important." My friends, to accept this invitation is more important than anything else in this world. There is nothing in the world that is so important as the question of accepting the invitation.

How many mechanics in this building have spent five years learning your trade in order to support your families and support yourselves a few years—forty or fifty years at the longest? How many professional men have toiled and worked hard for years to get an education that they might go out to the world and cope with it, and during all these years have not had a minute to seek their salvation? Is that a legitimate excuse? Tell Him tonight that you haven't time, or let this be the night—the hour—cost you what it will, when you shall say, "By the grace of God I will accept the invitation and press up to the marriage supper of the Lamb."

"Oh, but that is not my case," says another. "I have time. If I thought I could become a Christian I would sit here all night and let business and everything else go, and press into the kingdom of God. I am not fit to become a Christian; that's the trouble with me." He says: "Go into the highways and hedges," and "bring in hither the poor, and the maimed, and the halt, and the blind"—just invite them all, without distinction of the sect or creed, station or nationality. Never mind whether they are rich or poor. If the Lord doesn't complain about your fitness, you shouldn't look to see if you have the right kind of clothes.

I had to notice during the war, when enlisting was going on, sometimes a man would come up with a nice silk hat on, patent-leather boots, nice kid gloves, and a fine suit of clothes, which probably cost him a hundred dollars. Perhaps the next man who came along would be a hod-carrier, dressed in the poorest kind of clothes. Both had to strip alike and put on the regimental uniform. So when you come and say you aren't fit, haven't got good clothes, haven't got righteousness enough, remember that He will furnish you with the uniform of heaven, and you will be set down at the marriage feast of the Lamb.

I don't care how black and vile your heart may be, only accept the invitation of Jesus Christ and He will make you fit to sit down with the rest at that feast. How many are continually crying out, "I am too bad; no use of me trying to become a Christian." This is the way the Devil works. Sometimes he will say to a man,

"You don't want to be saved; you are good enough already." Then he will point to some black-hearted hypocrite and say: "Look at him and see how you appear in comparison; you are far better than he is." But, by and by, the man gets a glimpse of the blackness of his heart, and his conscience troubles him. Then says the Devil: "You are too bad to be saved; the Lord won't save such as you; you are too vile; you must get better before you try to get God to save you. And so men try to make themselves better, and instead, get worse all the time. The Gospel bids you come as you are. Seek first the kingdom of heaven—make no delay; come just as you are.

I heard of an artist who wanted to get a man to sit for a painting of the prodigal son. He went down to the almshouses and the prisons, but couldn't get one. Going through the streets one day, he found a poor, wretched man, a beggar, coming along, and he asked him if he would sit for the study. He said he would. A bargain was made and the artist gave him his address. The time for the appointment arrived, and the beggar promptly arrived and said to the artist: "I have come to keep that appointment which I made with you." "An appointment with me?" replied the artist; "you are mistaken: I have an appointment with a beggar today." "Well," said the man, "I am that beggar, but I thought I would put on a new suit of clothes before I came to see you." "I don't want you," was the artist's reply, "I want a beggar." And so a great many people come to God with their self-righteousness instead of coming in their raggedness. Why, someone has said, "It is only the ragged sinners that open God's wardrobe." If you want to start out to get a pair of shoes from a passerby, you would start out barefooted, wouldn't you?

I remember a boy to whom I gave a pair of boots, and I found him shortly after in his bare feet again. I asked him what he had done with them, and he replied that when he was dressed up it spoiled his business. When he was dressed up no one would give him anything. By keeping his feet naked he got as many as five pairs of boots a day. So, if you want to come to God, don't dress yourself up. It is the naked sinners God wants to save. Come to Him after you have cast off your self-righteousness and the Son of God will receive you.

I remember, some years ago, a man who had gone to sea. He led a wild, reckless life. When his mother was alive she was a praying mother. Ah, how many men have been saved by their mothers after they have gone up to heaven. Perhaps her influence made him think sometimes. When at sea, a desire of leading a better life came over him, and when he got on shore, he thought he would join the Freemasons. He made application, but upon investigation his character proved he was only a drunken sailor and was black-balled. He next thought of joining the Odd Fellows, and applied, but his application met with like result. While he was walking up Fulton Street one day, a little tract was given him—an invitation to the prayer meeting. He came and Christ received him. I remember him getting up in the meeting and telling how the Freemasons had black-balled him, how the Odd Fellows had black-balled him, and how Christ had received him as he was. A great many orders and societies will not receive you. But I tell you, He will receive you, vile as you are—He, the Savior of sinners—He, the Redeemer of the lost world—He bids you come just as you are.

Ah, there is another voice coming down from the gallery yonder: "I have intellectual difficulties; I cannot believe." A man came to me some time ago and said: "I cannot." "Cannot what?" I asked. "Well," said he, "I cannot believe." "Who?" "Well," he repeated, "I cannot believe." "Who?" I asked. "Well-I-can't-believe-myself." "Well, you don't want to." Make yourself out false every time, but believe in the truth of Christ. If a man says to me, "Mr. Moody, you have lied to me; you have dealt falsely with me." It may be so, but no man on the face of the earth can ever say that God ever dealt unfairly or that He lied to him. If God says a thing, it is true. We don't ask you to believe in any man on the face of the earth, but we ask you to believe in Jesus Christ, who never lied—who never deceived anyone. If a man says he cannot believe Him, he says what is untrue.

Ah, but there is another voice coming down from the gallery: "I can't feel." That is the very last excuse. When a man comes with this excuse he is getting pretty near the Lord. We have a body of men in England giving a new translation of the Scriptures. I think we should get them to put in a passage relating to feeling. With some people it is feel, feel, feel all the time. What kind of feeling have you got? Have you got a desire to be saved? Have you got a desire to be present at the marriage supper? Suppose a gentleman asked me to dinner. I say, "I will see how I feel." "Sick?" he might ask. "No; it depends on how I feel." That is not the question—it is whether I will accept the invitation or not. The question with us is, will we accept salvation—will you believe? There is not a word about feelings in the Scriptures.

When you come to your end, and you know that in a few days you will be in the presence of the Judge of all the earth, you will remember this excuse about feelings. You will be saying, "I went up to the Tabernacle, I remember, and I felt very good. Before the meeting was over I felt very bad. I didn't feel I had the right kind of feeling to accept the invitation." Satan will then say, "I made you feel so." Suppose you build your hopes and fix yourself upon the Rock of Ages; the Devil cannot come to you. Stand upon the Word of God and the waves of unbelief cannot touch you; the waves of persecution cannot assail you. The Devil and all the fiends of hell cannot approach you if you only build your hopes upon God's Word. Say, "I will trust Him, though He slay me—I will take God at His word."

I haven't exhausted all the excuses. If I had, you would make more before tomorrow morning. What has to be done with all the excuses is to bundle them all up and label them "Satan's lies." There is not an excuse but it is a lie. When you stand at the throne of God no man can give an excuse. If you have a good excuse, don't give it up for anything I have said; don't give it up for anything your mother may have said; don't give it up for anything your friend may have said. Take it up to the bar of God and state it to Him. But if you do not have a good excuse—an excuse that will stand eternity—let it go tonight, and flee to the arms of a loving Savior. It is easy enough to excuse yourself to hell, but you cannot excuse yourself to heaven. If you want an excuse, Satan will always find one ready for you.

Accept the invitation now, my friends. Let your stores be closed until you accept this invitation; let your households go until you accept this invitation. Do not let the light come, do not eat, do not drink, until you accept the most important thing to you in this wide world. Will you stay tonight and accept this invitation? Don't make light of it. I can imagine some of you saying, "Well, I never get so low as to make light of religion." Suppose I got an invitation to dinner from a citizen of Chicago for tomorrow and I don't answer it. I tear the invitation up. Would not that be making light of it? Suppose you pay no attention to the invitation tonight; is not that making light of it?

Would anyone here be willing to write out an excuse something like this: "The Tabernacle, October 29. To the King of Heaven: While sitting in the Tabernacle today I received a very pressing invitation from one of your servants to sit at the marriage ceremony of the Son of God. I pray you have me excused." Is there a man or woman in this assembly who would take their pen and write their name at the bottom of it? Is there a man or woman whose right hand would not forget its cunning and whose tongue would not cleave to their mouth if they were trying to do it? Well, you are doing this if you get up and go right out after you have heard the invitation.

Who will write this: "To the Lord of Lords and King of Glory: While sitting in the Tabernacle this beautiful Sabbath evening, October 29, 1876, I received a pressing invitation from one of your servants to be present at the marriage supper. I hasten to accept. "Will anyone sign this? Who will put their name to it? Is there not a man or woman saying down deep in their soul, "By the grace of God I will sign it." "I will sign it by the grace of God and will meet that sainted mother who has gone there." "I will sign and accept that invitation and meet that loving wife or dear child." Are there not some here tonight who will accept that invitation?

I remember while preaching in Glasgow an incident occurred which I will relate. I had been preaching there several weeks; the night was my last one, and I pleaded with them as I had never pleaded there before. I urged those people to meet me in that land. It is a very solemn thing to stand before a vast audience for the last time and think you may never have another chance of asking them to come to Christ. I told them I would not have another opportunity, and urged them to accept. I asked them to meet me at that marriage supper. At the conclusion I soon saw a tall young lady coming into the inquiry room. She had scarcely come in when another tall young lady came in; she went up to the first and put her arms around her and wept. Pretty soon another young lady came, went up to the first two, and just put her arms around them both. I went over to see what it was, and found that although they had been sitting in different parts of the building the sure arrow of conviction went down to their souls and brought them to the inquiry room.

Another young lady came down from the gallery and said, "Mr. Moody, I want to become a Christian." I asked a young Christian to talk to her, and when she went home that night, about ten o'clock—her mother was sitting up for her. She said, "Mother, I have accepted the invitation to be present at the marriage supper of the Lamb." Her mother and father lay awake that night talking about the salvation of their child. That was Friday night. The next day (Saturday) she was unwell, and before long her sickness developed into scarlet fever. A few days after I got this letter:

"Mr. Moody—Dear Sir: It is now my painful duty to

intimate to you that the dear girl concerning whom I wrote you on Monday has been taken away from us by death. Her departure, however, has been signally softened to us, for she told us yesterday she was 'going home to be with Jesus,' and after giving messages to many, told us to let Mr. Moody and Mr. Sankey know that she died a happy Christian.

"My dear sir, let us have your prayers that consolation and needed resignation and strength may be continued to us, and that our two dear remaining little ones may be kept in health if our Father wills. I repeated a line of the hymn—

'In the Christian's home in glory,
There remains a land of rest—'

"When she took it up at once and tried to sing,

'There the Savior's gone before me,
To fulfill my soul's request.'

"This was the last conscious thing she said. I should say that my dear girl also expressed a wish that the lady she conversed with on Friday evening should also know that she died a happy Christian."

When I read this I said to Mr. Sankey, "If we do nothing else we have been paid for coming across the Atlantic. There is one soul we have saved, whom we will meet on the resurrection morn."

Oh, my dear friends, are there not some here tonight who will decide this question? Do accept this invitation. Let sickness come, let sorrow come, you will be sure of meeting at the marriage supper of the Lamb. Blessed is he who shall be found at that marriage feast.

NOTES

Love's Last Appeal

James S. Stewart (1896–1990) pastored three churches in Scotland before becoming professor of theology at the University of Edinburgh (1936) and then professor of New Testament (1946). He was a professor who preached, a scholar who applied biblical truth to the needs of common people, and a theologian who made doctrine practical and exciting. He published several books of lectures and biblical studies including *A Man in Christ* and *Heralds of God*. His two finest books of sermons are *The Gates of New Life* and *The Strong Name*.

This sermon is taken from *The Gates of New Life*, published in Edinburgh in 1937 by T. & T. Clark.

James S. Stewart

3

LOVE'S LAST APPEAL

Mark 12:1–12

To READ THE parables of Jesus in the Gospels is to move through a wonderful picture gallery full of the most fascinating portraits—the Good Samaritan, the Younger Son, the Elder Brother, the Sower, the Shepherd, the Pearl Merchant, and many more—all painted by the hand of the great Master Artist. In one dim corner of the gallery, dim because the sunlight which falls upon the other pictures is here toned down and shadowed by a cross, hangs the Artist's self-portrait. Will you stand there with me for a few moments now, and let this picture speak to you?

For this parable, as Jesus told it, was sheer autobiography. And when you think of the Pharisees listening on the outskirts of the crowd that day as this vivid little tale unfolded itself, and seeing their own dark plots against Him (which they had imagined were utterly secret) suddenly and dramatically held up to the light before their very faces—when you think of that, do you not begin to feel that, of all the brave things Jesus ever did, the telling of this story was one of the very bravest?

But let us begin at the beginning.

Here was this lord of the vineyard. He bought his ground, planted his vineyard, fenced around it, dug troughs for the wine press, built a tower, put skilled husbandmen in charge. In short, he did everything conceivable—nothing was omitted or forgotten. Do you remember Isaiah's song of the vineyard? Jesus, steeped in His Old Testament, was remembering and quoting from it here. Listen! "My beloved hath a vineyard in a very fruitful hill; and he fenced it, and gathered out

31

the stones thereof, and planted it with the choicest vine, and built a tower in the midst of it, and also made a winepress therein; and he looked that it should bring forth grapes, and it brought forth wild grapes." And then God's great baffled cry: "What could have been done more to My vineyard that I have not done in it?"

Let each of us put this straight to his own soul today. What more could God have done for me than what He has done? "Oh," cries someone, starting up in protest, "He could have done far more! Look at my narrow lot. God could surely have given me more success, more opportunity, more power and skill and influence and talent, more of the good things of this world." Yes, perhaps He might. But is there not something deeper? "There is that soul I have made," God is saying, and He is looking at someone here as He says it. "Have I not given him a happy home and a task to work at; given him parents who prayed for him when he was a child, and friendship with its kindliness, and duty with its challenge; given him eyes to watch the sunset and the splendor of the dawn, ears to hear the glory of noble music, and hands to touch the hem of My garment everywhere; given him the Holy Bible to inspire and kindle his heart, and prayer to keep the road open to the mercy seat, and all the mystery and majesty of the cross of Christ. What more could I have done for him than what I have done?" That is the voice of God, our Creator and Redeemer. It is as though God were almost wondering whether He is to blame for the poverty of the result, whether there has been anything lacking on His part. "What more could I have done?" But today, hearing it, I for one can only answer, "Nothing, dear God, nothing! You have done everything, more than everything. It is I who am to blame that the fruit has been so meager."

And do you not feel that, too? One of the finest results that this hour of worship could possibly have would be that someone here, before today is done, should kneel down in that quiet room at home and say, with a meaning in the words that there had never been before:

> Spirit of purity and grace,
>   Our weakness, pitying, see;
> O make our hearts Thy dwelling-place,
>   And worthier Thee.

Look at the parable again and you will see here a picture of the marvelous patience of God. The lord of the vineyard sends first one servant, and he is beaten; then a second, and he is stoned; then a third, and he is killed; and then "many others." In spite of everything, he still keeps on sending them. That is Jesus' picture of Israel's story through the centuries—God sending one prophet after another, God pleading in voice after voice, always hoping that someday at long last His people would listen and repent. But it is not only the story of Israel. It is the story of the soul of man—very man.

When David, away back in the old days, fell into that dreadful disloyalty which smirched his whole career, Providence might have flung the man off, might have said, "I have done everything I could for him. I found him a shepherd and made him a king. I toiled night and day to fashion him into a leader of Israel and a saint, and after all that—this pitiful apostasy! It is heartbreaking. Throw him away!" When Peter and the other disciples began to fight about their stupid little questions of precedence in the very week of the Cross, just as though not one of them had ever been with Christ at all or felt His influence in the least degree, He might have wrung His hands in sheer despair. "You!" He might have cried, "you to be My witnesses and representatives and ambassadors! After three years with Me, you have not learned even the first rudimentary lesson, which is love, but act as if nothing I have ever said about this had really been meant at all. No, this finishes it! I am done with you. I will see things through without you." Was that it? If their Master had been anyone else but Christ, it would have been. But Christ was the incarnate patience of God.

And just think how patient God has been with you and me. Think how many chances He has given us. Think how often, when we have smothered one pleading voice within our heart, He has sent another. When we have stifled that, He has sent a third. When we have stoned that to death, He has kept on sending more and is not worn out with us even yet, but is perhaps sending another to someone here tonight. Think how often, when (as in Jeremiah's picture) the clay of which we are made has snapped and gone to pieces in God's hands, and when He would have been perfectly justified in throwing out such faulty material like rubbish on the scrap-heap, He has done nothing of the kind. Instead He has gathered up the fragments and started all over again, saying: "I must, I will make something fine and noble of this yet." Refusing to accept any rebuff, crying when we clench our fist and thrust it up into His face to strike Him, "Do it again, and again, and again, and I will love you still." Almost, in fact, plaguing us by His patience—it is so dogged and indomitable—frightening us, making us cry, "God, God, let go! Hands off—don't pester me!" Ah, says a psalmist, if we were to hide in very hell, God would come disturbing us even there. He loves us so much. Even when we cast Him off, His love keeps remembering happier days when we were truly His.

> I will not let thee go.
> The stars that crowd the summer skies
>   Have watched us so below
>   With all their million eyes,
>   I dare not let thee go. . . .
> I hold thee by too many bands:
>   Thou sayest farewell, and lo!
>   I have thee by the hands,
>   And will not let thee go.

It is to that patience of God, I know without a doubt, that I owe my life and soul. And has not His patience been marvelous with you?

Now notice another fact which Jesus has made very

vivid here: the way in which evil always tends to grow.
The husbandmen beat the first servant, but when the
second came they stoned him, and the third they killed.
There you have an instance of the natural and inevi-
table nemesis of evil. It grows and increases and mul-
tiplies itself. Sins apparently trivial open the door to
great ones, and these to greater still.

So Cain, in the old story, began with envy; then
envy became hatred; then hatred became murder. So
Peter had to deny Jesus not once, but thrice; and his
first denial was a low, muttered thing, ashamed of
itself—"I do not know Him." The second was more em-
phatic, "I tell you I don't know Him." The third was a
great, terrible shout, with oaths and curses, "Are you
all deaf? Can't you hear me? He is nothing to me—this
Jesus—I hate Him!" So in the first verse of the first
psalm, you have those three significant verbs, "walketh,
standeth, sitteth." "Blessed is the man that walketh
not in the counsel of the ungodly"—a mere casual glance
at sin in passing, for the man feels he does not really
belong to that environment, and so he just glances at
it, surreptitiously and half-ashamed and hoping no one
sees him. "Who walketh not," says the psalmist, "nor
standeth"—he has halted now, you see, for the sense of
shame is going, and he is growing bolder, and the thing
is beginning to assert itself, to grip. "Walketh, standeth,"
and then, finally, "sitteth," for the evil has him now,
and he is quite at home with it—fixed, rooted, and
settled, belonging to it body and soul!

That is sin's nemesis: it grows. In the very nature of
things, it is bound to grow. And again and again it has
happened that a man who began by being utterly
shocked at some sin, feeling a shudder pass over his
soul at the defiling contact of it, has ended by saying,
"Sin? Do you call it sin? I must say I cannot see anything very wrong about it." Yes, it grows. It is, as Thomas à Kempis said centuries ago, first a simple
suggestion, then a strong imagination, then delight,
and then assent. And you remember Thackeray's old
progression—an act, a habit, a character, a destiny.

That means that evil is never so easy to destroy as at its first attack. Then is the time for your soul's ultimatum. Don't wait, don't parley—be resolute, cast the tempting thought away. For if once you let it in, it will grow. It cannot help growing. So it was here. They beat the first servant, stoned the second, killed the third.

Follow the story further. Here is this lord of the vineyard, with all his messengers rejected and all his appeals refused. Luke's version of the parable at this point represents him as crying, "What shall I do?" Have you ever thought of that—God baffled, for the time being at least, by the blindness of His creatures? More than once the Scriptures hint at the possibility of that. Take that sudden, stabbing cry that breaks from one of Hosea's most moving pages: "O Ephraim, what shall I do unto thee? O Judah, what shall I do unto thee? For your goodness is as a morning cloud, and as the early dew it goeth away." What a picture of God wringing His hands, as it were, over His wayward children, of God—shall we dare to say it?—at His wits' end with men, baulked and thwarted and baffled and bewildered by that sheer dogged dourness that no appeal will move! So here in Jesus' story. "What shall I do?" cries the lord of the vineyard, "what shall I do?"

Then comes the great decision. "I will send My Son, My well-beloved Son. Surely that will move them! They will reverence My Son."

Will they? "We needs must love the highest when we see it," declares the poet: we cannot help ourselves, we are bound to love it, and to yield to it. Were Christ—so we confidently say—to come back in person to earth today, the whole world would be at His feet. There would be such a revival as has not been seen since Pentecost. Every church would be crowded, every knee bowed in adoration, every voice raised to hail Him King! But do you really think so? Carlyle suggested another possibility: if Jesus returned, He would be—not crucified, oh no! We are not barbarians now—lionized first, fêted and flattered, patronized and invited out to dine,

here, there, everywhere, and then—politely ignored!
For His demands for utter honesty and reality are still
as imperious as ever. When Jesus came back, said
Studdert Kennedy, the poet-preacher—for in imagination he had seen it happening—

> they simply passed Him by,
> They never hurt a hair of Him, they only let
> Him die;
> For men had grown more tender, and they
> would not give Him pain,
> They only just passed down the street, and
> left Him in the rain.
> Still Jesus cried, "Forgive them, for they
> know not what they do."
> And still it rained the winter rain that
> drenched Him through and through;
> The crowds went home and left the streets
> without a soul to see,
> And Jesus crouched against a wall and cried
> for Calvary.

"We needs must love the highest"; I wonder if that is
true. "They will reverence My Son"; I wonder if they
will. Let us narrow this down to the personal point.
God is looking at someone here. He is thinking of you.
"There is a soul," He is saying, "on whom I can count.
That soul, seeing My Christ, will be moved to the depths
of his being, will feel everything that is best within
him going down in full surrender, will forsake sin's
last clinging shadows, and stand up and live in the
light!"

Will you? For remember, Christ is God's last appeal.
Refuse this, and you refuse everything. "Having yet
therefore one Son, His well-beloved, He sent Him last
unto them." "Here is everything I am," declares God in
the Incarnation, "here in the fact of Jesus I have bared
to you My very heart." So that whenever a man faces
(as sooner or later he must) the question, "What shall I
do with Jesus?" he is facing life's ultimate challenge. If
this does not move us, nothing will. If Christ's love

does not break us down, God Himself can do no more. "They will reverence My Son." Will you?

It did not happen here. News reaches the rebel servants in the vineyard that another embassy is on the way. Then one of their own spies comes running in. "Do you know who it is?" he exclaims. "I have just heard! No ordinary servant this time—it is the heir, the lord's son!" And at that there is a clamor of voices. "His son? The heir?" Then, with a sudden gleam of devilment in their eyes, "Why then, this is our chance! As long as he is alive, we shall never be safe, never have this place for our own. But if only he were gone, we could do as we liked, live as we pleased, and have no one at all to trouble us. See! Yonder he is on the road. We must act—now. Come, let us kill him!" And so when the fearless young messenger arrives, they surround him, set upon him, strike him, fling him down, crush him, trample and batter the life out of him. Then they throw the poor dead mangled body outside the vineyard gate.

Just a story, was it? No—but autobiography. For within three days from the telling of the story, the whole thing actually happened. Word for word, the tale came true. For here were Caiaphas, Annas, and the rest, accredited keepers of God's vineyard. And here was the rumor flying around—"No ordinary prophet, this Man from Nazareth; greater than a prophet, the Lord's Son!" And here were men obsessed with the thought, "As long as He lives—this Jesus, this incarnate challenge of God—we shall never be safe. There is going to be no peace for us in our sins until He has been gagged, silenced, and hurried away out of sight. Come, let us kill Him!" And they did.

And they are doing it still—trying to silence Jesus. They will always be doing it. For Jesus is the most disturbing factor on the face of the earth at this moment. You can't sin in comfort. Christ is there. You can't feel free and happy in your sin—Christ's steady eyes are upon you. You can't call life your own—this stubborn Christ keeps haunting you. And sometimes a man, irked by these feelings and irritated by this Jesus whom he cannot shake off, grows almost desperate, and turns violent hands upon the conscience Christ has kindled within him. He chokes it, suffocates it, shakes the life out of it, and then flings the dead, useless thing away. "There now," he tells himself, "my life is my own at last! I can do what I like in peace."

But it does not work. For this surely is what the solemn close of the parable means—the final words of the story have the roll of thunder in them—that the most futile thing any man can do is to try to silence God.

Annas, Caiaphas, and the others might rub their hands on the day of Calvary, and say, "That settles Him! We shall hear no more of Jesus. Just look at Him hanging yonder, dead on His Cross. We have managed this well. He is finished!" Finished? Fools that they were! Everything about Him—His life, His influence, His work, His kingdom—had only just begun.

And if they, with Golgotha to help them, could not finish Jesus, no one else can. Stifle the inward voice as much as you please (and how often we do try to stifle it), silence it until you think it gone forever—and one day it will shatter the silence like a trumpet. Crush down the Christ who haunts you, bury Him beneath years of prayerlessness and neglect—and still He will resurrect Himself, and go marching through your soul. You are never done with Jesus. You have never heard the last of the Son of God. "Keep we our heads as high as we can," says Middleton Murry, closing his *Life of Jesus* (and he is no orthodox believer, but this is the final verdict to which his study of the fact of Christ constrains him) "keep we our heads as high as we can, they shall be bowed at the last." That is the truth. Heaven and earth shall pass away, but His words never. "Come, let us kill Him, and the vineyard will be ours." No, they killed Him once and He rose. They have killed Him a hundred times and a hundred times He has risen. And He is living tonight, and He is here. Of all strange delusions, the strangest, wildest, insanest, is to think that we can get rid of Jesus.

But happily we can finish on another note. Look at the vineyard again and imagine the scene now changed. The same servants are indeed still there—self-willed, bungling, unprofitable servants still. The road leading away across the hills is still there, the road to the land where the Lord of the vineyard dwells. Once more down the road a solitary figure can be seen moving. And now the servants (this time we ourselves are among them) have heard of His coming and know who the messenger is. It is the heir to the kingdom, the Son of the Lord. Now they are waiting for Him at the gates (and you and I are there), and one thought is filling every heart—"His Son? His only Son? Why then, how greatly He must love us—if, after everything, after all the sin and all the shame and all the way we have allowed His vineyard to run to waste, He still thinks us worthy of His Son! How hugely He must love us. If He loves like that, there must be now a new beginning, a new and uttermost dedication of mind and heart and will. We must love Him too."

And now can't you see that solitary figure on the road drawing near, almost at His journey's end, nearer and nearer—until the gate is reached? And then, what a shout it is that rends the skies! "This is the Heir; come, let us welcome Him! Son of the Lord of the vineyard, hail! This is the hour of new beginnings. Hearken, Jesus, to the vow we make—that never while this vineyard lasts, never while an ounce of strength abides in us, never while the memory of Calvary endures, never while life remains, and love and honor, and God's voice calling after us down the winds of all the days and all the nights of our existence—never will we break our troth to You. All hail, Son of the Lord!"

NOTES

The Unjust Steward

George W. Truett (1867–1944) was perhaps the best-known Southern Baptist preacher of his day. He pastored the First Baptist Church of Dallas, Texas, from 1897 until his death and saw it grow both in size and influence. Active in denominational ministry, Truett served as president of the Southern Baptist Convention and for five years was president of the Baptist World Alliance, but he was known primarily as a gifted preacher and evangelist. Nearly a dozen books of his sermons were published.

This sermon is taken from *The Salt of the Earth*, published in 1949 by Broadman Press.

George W. Truett

4

THE UNJUST STEWARD

Luke 16:1–12

ONE OF THE most arresting statements that ever came
from the lips of Jesus was spoken in connection with
the parable of the unjust steward. That parable is given
in the sixteenth chapter of Luke's gospel and was read
to you in the earlier moments of this service. This is
Christ's arresting and remarkable statement: "And I
say unto you, make to yourselves friends of the
mammon of unrighteousness: that, when ye fail, they
may receive you into everlasting habitations."

This parable of the unjust steward is the most chal-
lenging parable, in some respects, of all the parables of
Jesus. It has been the occasion for more comment, it has
provoked more perplexity, it has been more perverted
and abused, perhaps, than any other passage appearing
in the New Testament. The parable is a mighty exposure
of covetousness, and the great truths that Christ seeks to
impart would, if translated and applied worthily, make
for a glorious transformation of the whole earth. "And I
say unto you, make to yourselves friends by means of
your material property, much or little, that when your
property fails, as fail it will certainly when you die, then
these friends you have made, who have gone to heaven,
shall receive you into the eternal tabernacle."

Let us glance for a moment once again at this remarkable parable. The principal figure in it was a steward, just as was the trusted steward in Abraham's
household or as was Joseph in the household of
Potiphar. To this steward was entrusted the management of the affairs of his master, spoken of here as his
Lord, a term applied yet in many sections of the world
to men of high position.

43

This steward had abused his stewardship. He misused his position. He defaulted with his trust, and the knowledge of such defalcation reached the lord of the property and he summoned the steward before him. "What is this I hear of thee?" said the lord of the property. "Give an account of thy stewardship, for thou canst no longer be steward." All overborne, the defaulting steward went his way and had this soliloquy with himself. "What shall I do? The Master means to put me out of my stewardship, what shall I do? I cannot dig, I am above getting out in the hot sun and digging, and I am ashamed to beg."

So the steward said to himself: "This will I do. I will call all the debtors of my lord at once to me, and I will do them a favor so that when I get turned out, they will do me a favor. I will go through a piece of bribery, and when I lose my job here, they will take me into their houses." So to the first debtor he said: "How much do you owe my lord?" He said, "A hundred measures of oil." And he said to him, "Sit down quickly and write fifty on the bill." And to another he said: "How much owest thou unto my lord?" He said: "A hundred measures of wheat." He said "Write eighty," and so on and on. Now, when the lord of that property discovered what his steward had done, the Scriptures say that he commended the steward, not because he was a thief, but because he was clever and shrewd and had provided for his future. That is the story.

Thus Jesus said concerning the provision the steward had made for his own future security, "For the children of this world are in their generation wiser than the children of light." Jesus does not approve the steward's conduct. He simply states that what happened is happening all along in the world.

There is an old adage which says: "It is lawful to learn from your enemy." Jesus says: "We are to be wise as serpents." He does not mean that we are to sting and be poisonous and be venomous like serpents, but in certain respects we are to be "wise as serpents, and harmless as doves." He turns from this very worldly

incident and draws lessons from it and makes application of truths tremendous. "I say to you, make to yourselves friends by the means of your material property,
that when this property fails you, when it is taken out
of your hands, when by a reversal of circumstances,
and certainly when you come to die, you shall leave it
all. When this property shall fail you, these friends you
have made, who have gone on to the glory world, shall
welcome you into the eternal tabernacle." Those whom
you have helped can in turn help to give you "an abundant entrance" into the heavenly home. Jesus here
teaches a lesson from this story of the unrighteous
steward of untold moment for us all. May we learn
something of its high and vital meaning this very hour!

Jesus means to teach here, definitely, positively, that
our money may be made an immeasurable blessing to
us and to others, if it shall be wisely and worthily
used. Jesus teaches that it can add to our blessedness
and to our reward, not only in time but in eternity, if
we use this money as we should. Certainly, we should
like to know what Jesus' view is about our money.
Whether we have much or little, His view is important
to us.

Jesus does not leave us in the dark as to His view on
many questions. We have His teaching concerning the
great matter of personal salvation. He teaches that all
are lost, and that we must each be born again if we are
to be saved—born from above, born by the regenerating
power of the Holy Spirit. We have His teaching that
Christ's church is a democracy, a fraternity of brothers
and sisters, not an autocracy, but a democracy, without
disenfranchisement against any on account of age or
nationality or condition. We have His teaching that
the ordinances are for those who have found Christ.
Baptism and the Lord's Supper are not for unbelievers
but for believers. We have His teaching about our
relation to citizenship and our relation to our fellow
humanity of our land and of all other lands.

It behooves us to look more earnestly into the
teaching of our Master in the gospels concerning money.

Here the truth flashes out right away from this parable that money can be made one of the best friends one can have in life, or one of the cruelest and most down-dragging enemies. A great and gracious friend, our property, much or little, may be made; or a cruel, debasing enemy our property may be made. It is according to the way we acquire our property, and according to the way we use it when we get it, that makes it an asset or a hindrance.

Jesus shows us all that in this parable which I have just read you. Nowhere does Jesus put His condemnation on the man who has money. You do not find that in the Bible. He nowhere condemns a man because he has money. One of the rich men of the world was Job, and he was marvelous in his devotion to God. One of the rich men of the Old Testament was Abraham, and he was called the "friend of God." You might give all men today the same amount of property, and in a short time a few men would have most of it, because some are shrewder, are more clever, have more innate capacity than the masses have. What Jesus condemns is the wrong acquirement of property and the wrong use of property. Men with property will have to answer to God for the way they get it, and then for the way they use it after they get it. Jesus spoke out clearly on that point.

A man can take different attitudes toward money. He can take the attitude of utterly ignoring it. He can go away into a monastery, living there quietly, eking out his life as far away as he can get from people and from property and from the world's great battlefields and from the high demands of life. Surely you would not want that kind of life. The most laborious toil is preferable to that.

On the other hand, one can fall into the habit of bowing down to property, of worshiping property, for the covetous man is an idolater. This, the Bible distinctly teaches. His money has mastered him. It has perverted his powers, it has strangled him, it has suffocated him. He does not have the right views. His attitude is all wrong. Man can take the wrong attitude toward money and let it be his master. Therefore Paul was able to tell us that "the love of money is the root of all evil."

We would not desire to take either of these positions. We would not want to ignore it and despise it and say: "I will not address myself to a vocation, to the making of a living." The Lord magnifies work. He insists that every man shall be a worker. He anathematizes idleness. We are to magnify work. We are to get out in the busy world and do our full part in the battle of life. We are not to yield before ease or money or property. We are never to allow our property to be our master, never. We are to keep the mastery.

What are we to do with our property? We are to make the right use of every dollar of it, for let us remember it is a trusteeship. Let us remember about the steward, the steward in our Scripture today was not the owner of the property he managed. You are not the owner of the property that is in your name. The Lord is the owner of every penny of it. You are simply the agent, the steward. You are not the possessor of it. The Lord is the owner, the possessor. It is a part of the trusteeship committed to you while you are down here for thirty or forty or seventy or eighty years in the earthly journey. We are to make the right use of property and are to remind ourselves that to trifle with any trusteeship is to invite serious consequences.

You may trifle with your health by abusing your body with down-dragging habits which will fill your days with untold misery. Nature calls you to account for your stewardship of your physical life. Even so a man may misuse his property. His neighbors may not call him to account. That is not their function. He has to reckon with One whose eye watches his every thought and motive and expression of behavior. He will answer to God.

The doctrine of stewardship is a great regulative principle of human life. The nation that fails to recognize its stewardship will go down. The organization that trifles with it will go down. The church may have vast buildings and a vast membership, but if it becomes proud and disobedient to God, with respect to its stewardship, serious consequences will come to that church. The family, also, and the individual member thereof, must render an account to God for the use or misuse that they make of property, be it much or little. Property is a part of our stewardship of life.

Jesus advised us to make friends through our property. The Bible has much to say about property. The accumulator of the property and the temporary owner of it are both called of God to remember: "It is the Lord thy God who giveth thee the power to get wealth." Friends, if the hand of the Lord were withdrawn from us, we would indeed make wrecks of our lives. Physical and mental destruction would be our lot. Remember, "It is the Lord thy God that giveth thee the power to get wealth," and all of our power comes from Him. We are His stewards. We are His trustees. We are His divinely appointed agents of all of our property, whether it be much or little. "He that is faithful in that which is least," said Jesus, "is faithful also in much." Jesus taught that the servant who is faithful over a few things will be made ruler over many things. The Bible has much to say about the right way to acquire property and the right use of it, and says it with great clarity and positiveness.

Here in this great parable, Jesus makes the plea that all of us should wisely turn our money into the making of friends. Of far more value than gold is a good friend. There are very practical ways to make friends of the "mammon of righteousness." Many people need financial help. Great institutions need endowment. Afflicted children need hospitalization. Boys and girls need college training to fit them for greater usefulness in life. Mission fields need workers. Money can aid all of these causes. Jesus advised the Rich Young Ruler not to hoard his wealth but put it in circulation for the betterment of mankind. Jesus taught: "Use your money rightly. Make friends through your money. Use it for human need and for the spreading of the Gospel in a lost world."

"To give is to live, to withhold is to die." Oh, the wretchedness of the covetous man! He is miserable when you talk to him about parting with his money. Think of a man—the agent of God, the trustee of God, the steward of God—to whom He has entrusted certain property, think of his being unhappy when he is required to give an account of his stewardship of that property, not a penny of which is his own or ever was or ever will be!

Jesus comes with His great word: "It is more blessed to give than to receive." If we had some man of great wealth in this church, and he should say to us: "Now, Pastor, you need not say a word about the finances of this church, I will pay every dime that your church wants paid and let these people go free," we would not even discuss it with him one second. He would do us indescribable damage. He would help stifle all the finer powers of our religious life. Giving is a grace that should be emphasized among, and practiced by, all Christians.

If someone should come along and say: "I will take care of the pennies that this child is going to give." It would be a mistake to accept his offer. That child is being taught the great God-given doctrine of stewardship. Beginning as a child by giving his five or ten cents a week, he is being grounded in the doctrine and in the practice of stewardship. One day he may have a great deal of property and he can endow a college, or help an orphans' home, or help build a hospital. He may send a group of boys and girls away to college who could never go unless some friend should put himself into the breach and help them go.

Jesus in this parable, perhaps as in no other, teaches the marvelous possibilities of property. It can make heaven itself greater, and the welcome there more abundant, and your reward in heaven sweeter by the right use of your property. Use it to make friends.

Think of people coming from Burma, from India, from Japan, from China, from darkest Africa, and from the islands of the sea, and think of them in heaven forever talking about those consecrated missionaries who left their own land to tell lost people about Jesus and His love. Did you help send those missionaries to heathen lands, and were you "fellow-helpers to the truth" that saved those souls who are waiting in glory to welcome their friends into the "eternal habitations"?

Consider for a moment the reward coming to the faithful steward. He may be a humble man, with little of this world's goods, or he may have millions like John G. and Mary Hardin, who poured their millions into our Baptist colleges, and into our hospitals and orphanages, and into other vital Baptist institutions. Oh, yonder in heaven, many will come and say: "This is the man; this is the woman who saw that I got through college, who saw to it that I did not die back in a remote country place for lack of worthy medical treatments." Eternity itself will be enlarged and glorified by the men and women down here who use their money as they ought to use it.

Have I said enough to you? I believe I have. Oh, I am anxious for the members of this church to be well-pleasing to God. My soul sickens at the thought that you could be covetous men and women. My heart fails at the thought that your behavior shall ever be such that the godless, cynical man of the world shall speak of you as misers, as a people who love their money better than they love the church of God or the Savior of mankind. How I do expect you, and pray God to give you, to be a great group of cooperative, sympathetic, humanity-serving, humanity-loving, humanity-lifting men and women from this place to the very ends of the earth!

Now, you will make the application of all I have said, will you not? Make the application, please!

I am asked all along: "How much do you think one ought to give?" Well, it is not for me to pass on what you should give. I can pass on what I must give. But the question is insistent: "What do you think a church member should give?" I think no Christian ought to be willing to give less than a tithe. I have not a doubt that there are Christians who ought to give half of their income, and I have not a doubt that there are other Christians who ought to give even more than that. "As God has prospered you" is the law laid down for us. The principle of giving is: "Lay by him in store as the Lord hath prospered him." "Let everyone of you, upon the first day of the week," everyone of you, the boy, the girl, everyone of you!

It was a touching thing when the noble leader of our young peoples' work said the other day in a large committee meeting, "I expect hundreds of young people in our training unions, everyone, to sign our budget card as a regular giver before the week is out." What a glorious outlook for our church that will be! With hundreds of our young men and women, boys and girls, each one in the morning of life, each one assuming the proper role as stewards in the kingdom and service of Christ, who can forecast the future scope of our church work?

And then here is the great army of women. When did they ever fail in a good cause? And now they are going to enlist their homes, their husbands, their children, themselves, and they will tell others about our great causes. And here are our men, robust, red-blooded, heroic men, adventurous men, men who would like to do something worthwhile. You can do something worthwhile. Every time you consecrate any of your property with the right motive, for Christ's causes, you will be doing something that is as tremendously worthwhile as can be told by word of man or angel. Let us all put our best into our Lord's work these days—our best.

The poet gave us the right words in the song *Our Best*, which we shall sing presently.

> Hear ye the Master's call,
>   "Give me thy best."
> For, be it great or small,
>   That is the test.
>
> Do then the best you can,
>   Not for reward,
> Not for the praise of man,
>   But for the Lord.

This time, one time, now, let us everyone do his best for the Lord.

The Foolish Rich Man

William Mackergo Taylor (1829–1895) pastored
Presbyterian churches in Glasgow and Liverpool before
transferring to the Congregational ministry in 1872.
In that year, he became pastor of the famous Broadway
Tabernacle in New York City. He remained there until
1892, when he was made Pastor Emeritus. He gave
the Lyman Beecher Lectures on Preaching at Yale in
1876 and 1886. Among his many volumes of published
sermons are *The Parables of Our Saviour, The Miracles
of Our Saviour, Moses the Law-Giver, Joseph Prime
Minister, David the King of Israel, Peter the Apostle,*
and *Paul the Missionary.* Taylor's sermons represent
classic Scottish exposition at its best.

This sermon is taken from *The Parables of Our
Saviour,* published in London in 1886 by Hodder and
Stoughton.

William Mackergo Taylor

5

THE FOOLISH RICH MAN

Luke 12:13–21

THE CHARACTER OF a man is often indicated by the direction which his thoughts take when he is listening to a religious exhortation. Commonly, indeed, the speaker gets all the blame if he cannot hold the attention of his auditors to the subject which he desires to impress upon them. But, frequently, the true cause is to be found in the fact that the soul of his hearer is enthralled by some overmastering passion. Here, for example, the greatest of all preachers, even the Lord Jesus Christ Himself, while speaking of such important matters as the danger of hypocrisy, the comfort that comes from the knowledge of the universality of the providence of God, and the duty of confessing the truth before men, relying on the promised help of the Holy Spirit, is interrupted by the outburst of one of the company to this effect: "Master, speak to my brother, that he divide the inheritance with me." The topic thus introduced had nothing whatever to do with those which the Lord had just been handling. The interruption, therefore, was unseasonable. It was even impertinent, inasmuch as it thrust the personal squabbles of individuals about property on the attention of those whom He wished to think of topics immensely more important. It was, besides, an attempt to traffic in the eminence which Christ had acquired as a teacher by enlisting Him on the side of one of the disputants in a family quarrel, much as men in prominent positions nowadays are pestered with applications from every quarter to give their influence to enterprises which are to profit individuals who care nothing for them, save that they think they can make something out of their names and position.

53

It was, therefore, with some degree of severity that the Lord replied, "Man, who made me a judge or a divider over you?" There were properly constituted tribunals in existence for the settlement of all such disputes, and to them the complainant might apply. The Lord had no jurisdiction in the case. He was not authorized by those who alone could give Him the position of a judge to deal with such matters; and if He had consented to take action in them, He would have been held as setting Himself up as the rival and antagonist of the legal courts of the land. Therefore, just as He declined to settle categorically the question about tribute, He here refused to listen to the complaint which had been so intrusively thrust upon His attention. It was no part of His mission to meddle directly with legal or political affairs. He came for the regeneration of individuals, and through that alone did He desire or design to affect the public life of the nation. Therefore He would be no judge in such a matter as this man brought before Him. The man might, or might not, have right on his side: the courts would determine that. But whether he had or not, one thing was clear, the mere making of this demand by him at such a time, and in such a manner, showed that he was moved by covetousness. So, rising from the individual case, the Lord addressed Himself to the evil of which it was a manifestation. Turning to the multitude, He said to them, "Take heed, and beware of every form of covetousness"—for so, according to the best manuscripts, the clause should be read.

But what is covetousness? It is not simply the desire of property, for that is one of the instincts of our nature. The effort to acquire wealth plays a most important part in the education at once of the individual, the nation, and the race. At first, indeed, such is the influence of our depravity that the desire for property may develop the direst selfishness. But it is undeniable that, in proportion as a people obtains it, it rises both morally and socially. Where no property exists, you have neither laws, literature, civilization, nor religion.

The attempt to acquire riches stimulates frugality, develops forethought, and encourages that kind of self-denial which subordinates present enjoyment to future good, while, again, the possession of property leads to the respect of the rights of others. So close, indeed, is the connection between these two things, that, wherever property ceases to be respected, there you have an end of law, and an absolute reign of anarchy and terror.

The desire of property, therefore, with a view to its right and legitimate use, is not only not covetousness, but is lawful and right. As Robert Hall has said, "If there were no desire for wealth, there would be no need of it. It would soon cease to exist at all, and society would go back to a state of actual barbarism." Covetousness, therefore, is neither the having of money nor the desire to have it for the uses to which it may be rightly put; it is the desire of having money simply for the sake of having it—making that which is at best a *means* of ministering to life or comfort or enjoyment or usefulness into the great *end*.

Now, there is always a danger in our depraved natures, lest we should allow that which ought to be kept subordinate to become the controlling motive of our existence. Because money is so closely identified with our daily lives and so needful for the supply of our common and ordinary wants, that danger is especially great in reference to its acquisition. The fact that in our modern society a man is too frequently estimated by the magnitude of his wealth only increases the peril, so that we have peculiar need of the warning, "Take heed, and beware of every form of covetousness." This simply means, beware of setting up the possession of property or riches as the chief good to which everything else is to be made subservient. Let not the acquirement of wealth become the absorbing ambition of your life. Set not your heart on possession as the great object of your desire. Do not live simply to make money and hoard it up, but use what property you may acquire for the promotion of those higher and more spiritual ends, the attainment of which ought to be the great aim of your existence.

That is the meaning of the Savior's caution, and He enforces it with this consideration: "For a man's life consisteth not in the abundance of the things which he possesseth." The clause thus rendered is, in the original, somewhat involved, and is rather difficult to translate. It is thus given literally in the margin of the Revised Version: "For not in a man's abundance consisteth his life from the things which he possesseth." Some have taken it to mean that a man's life does not depend on the surplus of what he has above what he needs, while others would take it as denoting that life, in its higher sense, does not consist in possession, but in character. In the former case, the words simply enunciate the truth that little is needed to support life, viewed as mere animal being and well-being. As William Arnot has expressed it in his little volume on *The Race for Riches*: "A very small portion of the fruit of the earth suffices to supply a man's necessities. The main elements are a little food to appease hunger, and some clothing to ward off the cold. These, as a general rule, the poor man obtains; and what more can the rich consume? In this matter God has brought the rich and the poor very near to each other in life, and at death the slight difference that did exist will be altogether done away." This is doubtless, in the main, true. It accords readily enough with some aspects of the teaching of the parable which the statement on which we are now commenting was meant to introduce. But still it seems to me to fall sadly beneath the high level of our Lord's general treatment of the subject of life, and therefore I greatly prefer the other interpretation.

Life, in all its breadth and depth of significance, as the proper exercise and enjoyment of a rational, spiritual, and immortal being, such as a man is, does not consist in possession, but in character. The true riches are the riches of the soul toward God. "A man's life," as distinguished from that of a beast, does not depend on wealth. His happiness, his usefulness, his honor, may be secured without riches. Before God, he is estimated by what he is, rather than by what he has. Money is not the chief good. There are many things which it cannot purchase, but which yet may be acquired and possessed by those who are poor in this world's possessions. Of this sort are health, happiness, character, usefulness, and especially that acceptance with God, that relationship to Christ, "in knowledge of whom standeth eternal life," which we call salvation. There are wealthy men who are destitute of all these things, and there are many among the poor who possess them all, being "rich in faith, and heirs of the kingdom of heaven." With a fact like that before us, therefore, we can easily see that "a man's life," in its noblest sense, as the life of one worthy to be called a man, "consisteth not in the abundance of the things which he possesseth."

Now, it was to illustrate and enforce this truth that the Lord spoke the parable of the foolish rich man. The story is in itself so plain as to need little or no explanation. A certain landowner, already possessed of so much that he is called a rich man, saw an unusually large crop upon his fields and began at once to consider how he should dispose of it. He had no thought, indeed, of doing anything with it but keeping it to himself. But even to do that, he felt that he would require larger accommodation than he possessed. So he determined to pull down his barns and build greater. Then, as if already his purpose had been carried out, he rejoiced in anticipation over the "good time" which he would have, for he exclaimed, "I will say unto my soul, Soul, thou hast much goods laid up for many years; take thine ease, eat, drink, and be merry." But alas! He had forgotten to take God into his reckoning. At the very time when he was gleefully calculating on this future enjoyment, the decree came forth from the Eternal, "Thou fool, this night thy soul is required of thee; then whose shall those things be which thou hast provided?" That is the story, and the Lord adds the moral thus: "So"—that is, such a fool, and so great—"is he that layeth up treasure for himself, and is not rich toward God."

The essence of the lesson, thus, is the folly of this

rich man. Therefore the true interpretation will be found
in the answer to the question, Wherein did his folly
consist? To the consideration of that question, therefore, let us now address ourselves.

And here, in the first place, the folly of this man
appears in the fact that he completely ignored his
responsibility to God in the matter of his possessions.
He speaks of *"my* fruits" and *"my* goods," and the Lord
describes him as laying up treasure *"for himself."* No
doubt he had cultivated his ground and sown his seed;
but, after all, the greatest factor in the production of
his wealth had been God, who had sent his rain and
sunshine and so caused his crops to grow luxuriantly.
Yet he speaks throughout as if he had all the merit of
his prosperity and gives God no praise, while the idea
that any portion of the increase of his fields belonged
to God seems never to have entered into his mind. But
does this man stand alone in this particular? Are we
not all too sadly in the same condemnation with him?
How many among us glory in the fact that they are, as
the phrase is, self-made men? Have we never heard
the boast in the mouth of a successful merchant that
he is the architect of his own fortune? And are we not
all too prone to take to ourselves the sole credit for any
property we have acquired, or for any eminence we
have reached? Yet it is just as true in every department
of life, though perhaps not quite so apparent as it is in
agriculture, that the chief factor to success in it is God.
He gave the original aptitude and ability to the man;
His providence furnished the means of cultivating both
of these and opened up the avenues to prosperity. It
will commonly be found that the critical turning-points
of life that led directly to the results over which we
felicitate ourselves were due entirely to Him and came
altogether irrespective of our own arrangement. Why,
then, should we take the whole credit to ourselves?
Would it not be more appropriate for us to say, "Not to
us, O Lord, not to us, but to Your name give glory, for
Your mercy and for Your truth's sake"?

But the restriction to himself of the honor of his

success led directly to the complete appropriation by this man of its fruits. He regarded them as exclusively his own. He acted as if he felt that God had no claim to any part of them whatever. Far from looking upon himself as God's steward, he took everything for himself. Therefore he never thought of consulting God about the disposal of his property. He asked no advice of anyone. He simply "spoke with himself." "My goods are my own, and I shall do with them as I please," was the language of his heart. Whereas, if he had been animated by a right spirit, he would have said, "My fruits are Yours, O God. Show me what You would have me to do with them."

Now, am I uncharitable when I say that there are too many in these modern times who resemble the man in the parable in this also? Multitudes never pray to God about their business at all. Some may pray that He would send them prosperity; but when the prosperity comes, how few there are, comparatively speaking, who lay their wealth at His feet and ask Him to direct them in disposing of it! Disposing of it! Alas, that is the last thing they ever think of. Their one aim is to keep it, and, if possible, to increase it. Accumulation is their great ambition; and if they spend at all, they spend, too many of them at least, on their own indulgence, and not in the furtherance of those good and noble objects with which the glory of God and the welfare of men are identified. We cry out against those defalcations on the part of trusted officials in banks and other commercial houses which have been so frequent among us in recent years. I would not say a single word either in vindication or in extenuation of such iniquity. It is as wicked as it is said to be and deserves the severest punishment. But how many of those who are loudest in its condemnation are themselves guilty of similar defalcation before God, inasmuch as they have kept for themselves and spent on themselves the wealth which He has entrusted to them for the welfare of others and the glory of His name?

The creed of the communist is the extreme protest

against this extreme of selfishness, and, like all other extremes, it is itself as bad as that against which it protests. But if the New Testament doctrine of stewardship was universally acted upon by those who are possessed of property, communism would cease to exist. Property has its responsibilities as well as its rights; if its responsibilities were more fully acted on, its rights would be more sacredly respected. The communist says to the capitalist, "What is yours is mine, and I will come and take it by force." That is theft. But the Christian says, "What is mine is *God's*; and I will use it, under His direction, for the good of others." That is stewardship; in that alone is the antidote to the troubles which have so long agitated the countries of the Old World, and which are making their appearance now among ourselves. It is an awful folly for the man of wealth to ignore his responsibility to God for the use which he makes of his wealth.

But, in the second place, the folly of this man appears in the fact that he ignored the claims of other men upon him for his help. He had no idea, apparently, that there was any other possible way of bestowing his goods than by storing them in his barns. As Augustine, quoted by Trench, has replied to his soliloquy, "Thou *hast* barns—the bosoms of the needy, the houses of widows, the mouths of orphans and of infants"; these are the true storehouses for surplus wealth. It is right to provide for those who are dependent upon us; it is prudent to lay up something in store against a possible evil day. But after that, the storehouse of wealth should be benevolence. By scattering it in useful directions, it will be most effectually preserved. There are not a few among us today who, in the reverse of fortune that has come upon them by recent disasters, can say, "I have still at least that which I gave away. It was given to the Lord, and He has taken care of that."

I have somewhere read that a lady once went to call upon a friend near the close of autumn, and found her emptying her closets, exclaiming, "Oh, these moths! These moths! They have consumed almost everything that I laid away in the beginning of the summer." The visitor expressed her sorrow, but said she did not know what it was to have a garment moth-eaten. Whereupon her friend asked for the specific which she used and to her surprise received for answer, "I gave away to the poor months ago all the garments for which I had no longer use; and there was no difficulty in preserving the remainder from the moths."

The true storehouse for our surplus is benevolence. That is a barn which is large enough for all that we can put into it. Rightly bestowed in that barn, our treasures are where "neither moth nor rust doth corrupt, and where no thieves break through to steal." Benevolence clips the wings of riches so that they do not fly away; while, at the same time, it sweetens the breath of society, and deprives the agitator of the stock in trade wherewith he infuriates the "sand-lot" audience to deeds of violence and confiscation. He who has is, in a very important sense, a debtor to him who has not. As I have elsewhere said, "What I have that another has not is to be used by me, not for my own aggrandizement, but for the good of that other, as well as for my own. It is committed to me as a trust, and is to be expended by me for the benefit of others as well as for myself.

"The greatness of exceptional endowment, of whatever sort it may be, carries with it an obligation to similar exceptional greatness of service. This is the Gospel principle. It makes the powerful man the protector of the weak; the rich man, the provider for the poor; the learned man, the teacher of the ignorant; and the free man, the emancipator of the enslaved. Thus, by so much the wealthier a man is, if he acts on this principle, it will be just so much the better for the poor, for whom he is a trustee." That is the only principle that can preserve us from constant upheaval between class and class in society. They who ignore it are not only dishonoring God, but are foolishly furnishing the fuse for unscrupulous men to use in the production of some dynamite explosion that may shake the nation to its center.

But, in the third place, the folly of this man is seen in the fact that he imagined that material things were proper food for his soul. The mere animal life of the body may be supported by such goods as this man was about to lay up, but the soul needs something better than these. Its true food is God Himself; and hence Jesus, in the moral of the parable, calls the man who has that "rich toward God." The psalmist tells us that when the Israelites lusted after flesh to eat, "[God] gave them their request; but sent leanness into their soul" (Ps. 106:15)—words which plainly imply that while the body may be pampered with its material food, the soul may be really starving. So, again, in reply to Satan, the Lord, quoting from Deuteronomy, said, "Man shall not live by bread alone, but by every word . . . of God" (Matt. 4:4). When His disciples, having left Him hungry, came back to the well and could not get Him to eat, He replied, "I have meat to eat that ye know not of. . . . My meat is to do the will of him that sent me, and to finish his work" (John 4:32, 34). That is the true food of the soul. All else for it is worse than the husks which the swine did eat were to the prodigal.

But we may get at the same conclusion in another way. Thus we speak of a man's being rich in intellectual resources, meaning thereby that he has the means of satisfying, to a large extent, the cravings of his mental nature. When we say of another that he is deficient in intellectual resources, we wish it to be understood that he has in himself nothing to fall back upon in the hour when he is cut off from all material delights. Now, carrying this mode of speech up to that moral and spiritual department that is the highest in our complex humanity, we see at once that he is rich who has a good conscience, a will in unison with God's, and joy in the contemplation of Jehovah, while he is poor whose soul is burdened with a sense of guilt which he cannot remove, and whose heart is filled with horror and dismay at the prospect of standing naked and open before the eyes of Him with whom he has to do. True riches—or, in other words, the true food of the soul by which alone it can be nourished and satisfied—are to be found in God alone. Reconciliation to God, peace with God, likeness to God, and fellowship with God— that alone can fill the heart of man. God for us in the work of His Son, God with us in the orderings of His providence, God in us in the indwelling of the Holy Spirit, and God before us in the hope of heaven—that is the true food of the spirit of man. To think of sustaining it with material fruits and goods and possessions is as absurd as it would be to try to satisfy the hunger of the body with a diamond or to quench the thirst of the body with a pearl. As the poet has expressed it,

> Attempt, how monstrous and how surely vain!
> With things of earthly sort, with aught but God,
> With aught but moral excellence, truth, and love,
> To satisfy and fill the immortal soul.
> Attempt, vain inconceivably! attempt
> To satisfy the ocean with a drop,
> To marry immortality to death,
> And with the unsubstantial shade of time
> To fill the embrace of all eternity!

This was the folly of the rich man here. Let us take care that it be not also ours. "God has made us for Himself, and our souls must be ever restless until they rest themselves in Him."

But now, finally, the folly of this rich man is apparent from the fact that he had entirely ignored the truth that his material possessions were not to be his forever. When the decree went forth, "This night thy soul shall be required of thee," he could not prevent its being carried out. All his wealth could not bribe the death-messenger that came to summon his soul into the presence of its God or avail to lengthen his life on earth a single hour. And when he went, he could not take his riches with him. As the Spanish proverb has put it with a horrible distinctness, "There are no pockets in a shroud." "How much did he leave?" asked one man of another in the streetcar as they were talking of a millionaire whose death had been announced in the morning paper. *"All he had,"* was the solemn and suggestive answer. Let these two things stand out in lurid distinctness on this subject: wealth cannot buy off death, and when we die we can take none of it with us. Then you will understand how supremely foolish it is for a man to live simply and only for its accumulation.

But another thought is suggested here. Then "whose shall those things be which You have provided?" Ah, me! If some of those wealthy men who have gone in recent years from this busy, bustling city into the world beyond could come back for a moment and see what fightings there have been over their fortunes; how the details of their own idiosyncrasies have been dragged out into the light, to prove, if possible, that they had not sense enough to make their wills; how the most painful secrets of their lives have been proclaimed upon the housetop; how the skeleton in their closet has been handled and laughed over by the profane and unfeeling crowd; and how their sons and daughters and relations, out to the farthest limit of consanguinity, have wrangled over their portions—I think they would say within themselves, "What consummate fools we were to spend our days on earth in laying up treasures to be squandered thus in the courts, and to be quarreled over by a hungry crowd, as wolves howl over carrion!" And if they had to live again, they would try, I think, to be their own executors, and to use their possessions in a way that would bless the world and glorify their God. There has been, as I cannot help thinking, a grim irony in God's providence in cases like these; and as I read the reports of the surrogate's court from time to time, I am reminded of the words, "He that sitteth in the heavens shall laugh; the Lord shall have them in derision." At all events, they prove conclusively the shortsightedness and folly of those whose sole delight in life was the adding of dollar to dollar.

But a deeper thought is here suggested: "Whose shall those things be?" Whose were they all along? They were God's, and should have been used for God. You remember in that most glorious scene in David's glorious reign, when he brought out what he had gathered for the building of the temple and consecrated it all to God, and his people willingly followed his example, he used these remarkable words: "All things come of thee, and of thine own have we given thee. *For* we are strangers . . . and sojourners, as were all our fathers: our days on the earth are as a shadow, and there is none abiding" (1 Chron. 29:14–15). Mark the force of that *for* in this connection. Men come and go, but God is the immortal owner of all things; in giving to Him of our possessions, we but give Him of His own. Friends, if there were more acknowledgment of that truth among us, there would be more liberality like that of David, and our missionary and benevolent societies which are continually laboring in the rearing of the great spiritual temple of His church would not be so often in straits with their balances so largely on the wrong side of the ledger. Think on these things, I beg of you, and the Lord give you understanding in all things.

We see now how the moral of this story is established. "So is he that heapeth up treasure unto himself, and is not rich toward God." The first great thing for us is to be rich toward God. That will keep us from giving undue importance to earthly treasure—no, it will teach us how to use that treasure and show us that we may keep it best by spending it for God. That is the gist of the whole matter.

I ought now, therefore, to proceed to consider the question of how these riches toward God are to be acquired and increased. Here, however, your time forbids me to enlarge. James gives one answer when he speaks of God as having "chosen the poor of this world rich in faith" (James 2:5); and Paul supplements his statement when he exhorts Timothy to charge them that are rich in this world, that they be "rich in good works" (1 Tim. 6:18). Faith in Jesus Christ enriches us by giving us the blessings of forgiveness, peace, holiness, and heaven. Good works, wrought as the outcome of gratitude for these blessings, enrich us with present happiness and future reward. These are things which the world cannot give or take away. These are things which are the possessions of our soul and of which death cannot deprive us. The one of them is a present heaven, and the other will be an enrichment of the heaven that is in the future. Lay up these treasures for yourself, then, for no power can take them from you. And if you make that spiritual accumulation your supreme care, covetousness will find no lurking place within your heart. The wealth of earth will be valued by you only for the good works which it will give you the means of performing, and so the gold that is material and uncertain may become, in a wondrous way, transmuted into the riches which are spiritual and abiding. Here is something better than the philosopher's stone, for it turns material gold into immortal riches.

NOTES

Disciples for Building and Battle

George Campbell Morgan (1863–1945) was the son
of a British Baptist preacher and preached his first
sermon when he was thirteen years old. He had no
formal training for the ministry, but his tireless
devotion to the study of the Bible helped him to become
one of the leading Bible teachers of his day. Rejected
by the Methodists, he was ordained into the
Congregational ministry. He was associated with
Dwight L. Moody in the Northfield Bible conferences
and was an itinerant Bible teacher. He is best known
as the pastor of the Westminster Chapel, London (1904–
1917 and 1933–1945). During his second term there,
he had Dr. D. Martyn Lloyd-Jones as his associate.

Morgan published more than sixty books and
booklets, and his sermons are found in *The Westminster
Pulpit* (Hodder and Stoughton). This sermon is from
the "Westminster Pulpit," a series of pamphlets
published by Westminster Chapel. The sermon was
preached Sunday evening, August 22, 1926.

George Campbell Morgan

6

DISCIPLES FOR BUILDING AND BATTLE

Luke 14:25–35

BELOW ARE TWO questions, both of them moving in the figurative realm, and we can only understand their value as we keep them in their context.

> Or what king, as he goeth to encounter another king in war, will not sit down first and take counsel whether he is able with ten thousand to meet him that cometh against him with twenty thousand?

> For which of you, desiring to build a tower, doth not first sit down and count the cost, whether he hath wherewith to complete it?

The paragraph is arresting for many reasons. The story in which it is found occupies, in the Gospel of Luke, chapters 14, 15, 16, and 17 so far as verse 10. In these chapters we have the account of a Sabbath afternoon in the life of Jesus; as a matter of fact, it is the last of which we have any account in the course of His ministry. It tells us how He accepted the invitation of one of the rulers of the Pharisees to eat bread with him, and going into the house of that ruler, He did perhaps the most unconventional things that He ever did. When He came out, Luke tells us that there went with Him great multitudes.

No man can read these narratives of the Life of Jesus without being impressed with the fact that everywhere He attracted men and women to Himself. I am not saying that they all obeyed Him or that they crowned Him. I am only referring to His supreme and superlative attractiveness. When He left this house, evidently beginning to walk along the way, His face being set toward Jerusalem on the final journey, the people got up from where they had been waiting, and moved after Him. Luke tells us that He turned, and facing the crowd of people that were eager to follow Him, loving to be with Him, waiting to hear anything He might have to say to them, most keen to see any work that He might work, He uttered the terms of discipleship, the most searching and severe that ever fell from His lips.

I read them to you. I am not going to stay now to read them again, but you remember them. If we are perfectly honest, and of course we are going to be that in the house of God, we shall admit that as we read them or heard them read terror filled our hearts. Or were you not listening when I read them? Or were you imagining as I read them that you knew them, and therefore you could think about what you would do in the city tomorrow? That is the trouble, you know, with our worship. I never read them, as God is my witness, without wondering if I am a disciple at all.

He told that listening crowd that whereas they were attracted to Him, eager to follow Him, wanting to hear Him, loving to watch Him, desiring in some way to be identified with Him, it was impossible for any man to be His disciple unless that man should put His claims above the highest and holiest and best things of earthly life and relationship. I need not insult the intelligence of this audience by reminding you that when He speaks here of hating father and mother, wife, child, brother, sister, life, He is not saying that the necessity for discipleship is malice in the heart against such. He is simply indicating the fact not that low things and vulgar things are to be given up, but that high things and holy things and beautiful things, the most beautiful things of the world—love, the love of father, of mother, of wife, of child, of brother, and sister, and the love of life itself—if the hour shall ever strike when there is a conflict between loyalty to Him and these high loves, these are to be trampled underfoot.

Then He uttered the second of His terms of

discipleship. He said that no man can come after Him and be His disciple unless that man is prepared to take up his own cross and follow Him. Then He gathered up these two and said, "Except a man renounce all that he hath, he cannot be My disciple."

These are His terms of discipleship. You notice that I did not say they *were*. They *are*. They abide. Christ never told anyone that it was going to be easy to be a Christian. That blasphemy against eternal things is the outcome of a misunderstanding of Christ's message.

Between the enunciation of the two terms and their recapitulation in the form of one, I find the two verses I have read. He said, "Which of you, desiring to build a tower, doth not first sit down and count the cost, whether he hath wherewith to complete it? . . . Or, what king, as he goeth to encounter another king in war, will not sit down first and take counsel whether he is able with ten thousand to meet him that cometh against him with twenty thousand."

What did our Lord mean by these two questions and these two suggestions? He was appealing to His listeners, the men and women who were hushed into silence, and I cannot but believe, subdued and solemnized in great fear at His terms. To them He said, "Which of you going to build a tower, or what king going to make war." He was talking to His hearers, and I have no hesitation in saying, though I have not the authority for it is a documentary statement, that He saw upon the faces of that crowd exactly the protest that is in my heart when I hear these terms of discipleship. He knew what they were thinking.

I will try to interpret to you their thinking. They were thinking and saying in their hearts something like this: Oh, Jesus, prophet of Nazareth, we have followed You a long while. We love Your wonderful teaching; we love the tenderness of Your dealings with humanity. We would like to be identified with You, but we are filled with terror when You make Your terms of discipleship so severe! Why not make it easier for us? Why ask us to trample under foot the high loves of earth in order to be loyal to You, if necessary. Why ask us to take up the cross? Cannot it be easier? Is there not some easier way of discipleship than that? He saw the protest on their faces. He explained to the wistful crowd the reason for the severity of His terms. He said, "Which of you building a tower does not first count the cost? Which of you going to battle but does not consult as to the quality of his soldiers?" By which He did not mean that *they* were to count the cost. He never told men they were to count the cost. He told them they were to come after Him without counting the cost. They were to come at *all* costs, that if a man would come after Him, if his right hand offend, he must cut it off, or his eye cause him to stumble, he must gouge it out.

Then what did He mean? He meant that *He* had to count the cost. He was the builder. He was the warrior. He was appealing to these men to put themselves in His place, as though He had said to them, You are protesting in your heart against the severity of My terms. Do you not understand Me? Suppose you were in My place, which of you going to build a tower would not count the cost? Supposing you were in My place, which of you, as a king going to war, would not be concerned with the quality of your soldiers? My terms are severe because I want men and women as disciples who will stand by My side until the building is done, until the fight is won. That is the reason for the severity of His terms.

That being so, let us reverently consider some things revealed. First, we discover our Lord's conception of His own work in the world. That work, as suggested by His two figures of speech, is that of building and battle. That is consonant with the whole biblical revelation. Six months before this at Caesarea Philippi, when Peter made his great confession that Christ was the Son of the living God, Jesus said to him, "On this rock I will build My church [building] and the gates of Hades shall not prevail against it" [battle]. In other words, the mission of Christ is revealed suggestively in these figures of speech as being constructive and destructive. He came into the world for building, and because there are forces that prevent the building, He came into the world for battle.

If we stand back a little further from the record that we may have a larger view, we find that the whole story of the Bible is the story of God in human history—building and in battle. The constructive is the ultimate in the purpose of God, but the destructive is necessary in the process. The Bible opens in a garden. Where does it end? In a city. The Bible is the story of God's process from the Garden to the City. His determination to realize the ultimate meaning of humanity as it can only be expressed in the city. Man is also seen all the way trying to build his city, the passion for it being inherent in the human soul, but he has not yet built a city that is worth living in, not even London. Garden cities are approximating to the divine ideal, but there are no garden cities that are perfect yet, but they are going to be. God's city will be a garden city, and into that ultimate city all the nations shall bring their glory and their honor. It is only God-built, and all the way fighting is necessary, fighting against the obstructive forces that prevent or postpone the building of the city.

Charles Haddon Spurgeon called his magazine *The Sword and Trowel*. What made him do that? The idea was taken from Nehemiah, and he knew that in Nehemiah you have revelation of abiding principles. Nehemiah, in building the walls of the city, had a sword in one hand and a trowel in the other. So he built. Thus Nehemiah is a wonderful illustration of the work of God in the march of the centuries, ever building and always at war. Jesus came into the world and said on a memorable occasion, "My Father worketh hitherto and I work."

Christ is far more concerned in the fulfillment of God's enterprise in the world, with the quality of His disciples than with the quantity. "Let no man misunderstand me." If it be a matter of ultimate salvation, He is concerned with quantity, for God loved the world, and there is no human being outside the sweep and scope of the divine love or the purpose of the redeeming Lord. But He is seeking fellow-workers, and therefore He is far more concerned, I repeat, with quality than with quantity. We need either to discover this afresh, or to rediscover it. We are cursed today with a passion for statistics. I find it all around the world. People will say, "Look at this chapel tonight. That is a fine success." Not necessarily so. There are other chapels where only a handful of souls have gathered, and yet perhaps in the records of eternity we shall find that more mighty work for God is being done there than here.

In the Old Testament the story of Gideon is the particular illustration of this principle. Israel had been in cruel bondage to the Midianites. They had been disciplined by God because of their dereliction. The discipline having served its end, God had ordained their way of escape. He raised up Gideon. He called for an army and there reported thirty-two thousand men. Then there came from God that strange word that he had too many. Too many? Can God not use thirty-two thousand? That depends upon their quality. Gideon was ordered to proclaim to the army of thirty-two thousand that if any men were fearful they could go back home. Then there took place one of the most remarkable military movements in history. Right about face, quick march, twenty-two thousand going home. I am not afraid to apply that to the hour in which we live. I say to you Christian men and women: If you are fearful, if you are afraid, if you think perhaps that after all Jesus is going to be hounded out of the world and defeated in the enterprises of God and go down in defeat, for God's sake clear out of the ranks. God can do more with ten thousand in whose hearts there is no trembling than with thirty-two thousand, twenty-two thousand of whom are filled with panic.

But we are not through with our Old Testament story. Again the voice of God, I think, must have surprised the soul of Gideon. The people are yet too many. What now shall we do? These men are at war. The method of

Midian's fighting is the method of ambush. You need to know where Midian is or she will track you down. Bring these men to the water. They must have water. It is necessary to watch how they take it. He brought them to the water, and ninety-seven hundred fell to the ground in their eagerness for the necessary water, forgetting that they were soldiers, and went down on all fours and drank their fill. Three hundred only bent down, stooped for their water, still alert for the enemy. And God said, "With the three hundred that lapped I will save you. Send back home," said God, "all men who take unnecessary time for necessary things." How many of you will go home these days? How many of us will go home?

So the deep, profound question for us who name the name of Christ, who love Him in a certain way, who love to consider His words and to watch His works, to sing His hymns, is: How much am I worth to Him for His building and for His battle? I have sung, and sung honestly, and so have you—

> Thou, O Christ, art all I want,
> More than all in Thee I find.

That is what He is to me. What am I worth to Him? Supposing He fails, how much will you lose? If He is beaten, how much have you invested in His enterprise? That is the question of all questions. Which of you going to build would not count your cost? What king going to war does not consult concerning the quality of his soldiers.

So let us look at these terms for a moment. The first, I will read again:

> If any man come after Me, and hate not his father,
> and mother, and wife, and children, and brethren,
> and sisters, yea, and his own life also, he cannot
> be My disciple.

We are shrinking, we are saying that this is a terribly severe test. It certainly is. And yet is it? Is it not almost too late in the day to call that severe.

I cannot stand in this pulpit without the most

poignant and shattering memories of my life crowding back upon me. I remember that August day in 1914, myself personally a broken man, I had escaped to the sea for rest at Mundesley and there came the crack of doom. I came back and my staff gathered back around me. I had got some rooms here, and I went up there the first night and tried to sleep. I could not sleep. I got up and stood and I watched them going. I watched them while they went by. Every night they went on, they went on, day after day, week after week, month after month, until five million of our boys went without conscription. I can hear them yet. The tramp of the men as they went, singing "Tipperary" sometimes. Did not these boys love father and mother? How they loved them! Did not these boys love wife and the little children who waved to Daddy as he went? How they loved them! Did not these boys love their brothers and their sisters? How they loved them! Did not these boys love life, this glorious life? How they loved it, beautiful life. But oh, my God, an hour had struck when something bigger than love of father and mother and wife or child, brother or sister called them. I can still hear the tramping of their feet through the night. Tramping! Tramping! Tramping! Tramping! Christ only asks of His people that they shall be as loyal to Him as the boys who followed in that appalling hour of our travail and our agony.

There are some hymns which sometimes I feel it is almost a mockery to sing.

> Onward, Christian soldiers,
> Marching as to war.

What do we know about war? Have we got any scars of battle? Have we ever been weakened by the way in the world's agony? I am not saying you have not, beloved. I am saying, have we? When the call of Christ comes, do we trample underfoot love and all high things when they conflict with loyalty to Him? Are we true to Him? Are we prepared to be? These are the men and women that He wants. It is almost a vulgar thing to say of

God, and still I say, God but asks of the men and women who constitute His sacramental host and bear His name that they have the same spirit that actuated the boys as they went twelve years ago.

We pass to the next statement, in which He said,

> Whosoever doth not bear his own cross, and come
> after Me, cannot be My disciple.

What is it to bear the cross? I have no desire to use rough language, but a great deal of nonsense is talked about concerning cross bearing. Or if that be rough, let me put it in another way. There is a great deal of unintelligent observation made on cross bearing. I will tell you exactly what I mean. I hear Christian men or Christian women, Christian people, talking of their physical suffering, of their mental anguish, by reason of certain difficulties and obstacles, as though they constituted the cross. These things are not the cross, these things are never the cross. We have not touched the realm of the cross, when our suffering is peculiar to ourselves. These things may be His discipline, they may be His wonderful methods of preparing us for larger life, but they are not the cross.

The cross had one meaning and one meaning only. The cross is always personal, self-emptying, in order to effect the serving and the saving of others. You and I know nothing of the cross so long as our suffering is merely personal. But God forbid that should seem to be saying a hard thing. My heart is in sympathy with yours in your sorrow; but our personal sorrows do not constitute the cross, unless our sorrow is the result of a self-emptying in order that others may be served and somebody else may be saved.

What is the cross? My dear sister, member of the Christian church, in all the graciousness of your character, do you know anything about the cross? I am not questioning your worthiness. What are you doing? You are a member of the Ladies' Dorcas Guild or Sewing Circle. You give regularly and you stitch garments for the poor. Great work, beautiful work! But that is not the cross. But do you remember one day when in your life compassion surged and flamed and you violated the conventionalities of society and trampled upon your own fine sensitiveness and took to your arms a soiled, smirched woman. That cost you something. That is the cross!

I think back to Ancoats, Manchester, many years ago, when the great saint Francis Crossley, whom Dr. Alexander Maclaren called Saint Francis of the Manchester slums, said a curious thing to me as we sat talking into the night after a meeting. He said to me, "Morgan, I shall never forget when first I learned the luxury of giving. I first learned the luxury of giving when giving cost me something. It was when General William Booth was just starting his Darkest England scheme. He came down here to Manchester to address a meeting. I was sympathetic and promised to be present on the platform, and before I went I wrote a check for £1,000 to put on the plate. As that prophet-evangelist portrayed the submerged tenth, I crushed my check in my hand. I was so ashamed of it. I went home to this room where we are sitting tonight and faced it out that I was going to give what I would not miss. I opened my desk and took my bank book and recast everything, and before morning I had put into the post a check which meant that for one year, at least, and more, I had to know every day the principle of sacrifice."

The luxury of the cross! Strange paradox, but tremendous truth. My dear friend, church member, church officer, it may be minister, what do you know about the cross? Our Lord says He wants men and women who can share His sufferings, make up that which is behind-hand in His sufferings, know the fellowship of His sufferings, men and women of the cross. How much are we worth to Him?

I am not going to ask for any answer. I do not think that any answer given in a crowd would be worth listening to. I am going to make no answer. But this Sabbath evening service will not be lost if, when we get home, somewhere quietly in the inner chamber with the door shut, altogether careless of human opinion—that damnable thing that paralyses us so often—and in the presence of our Lord, we find out what we are worth to Him. If the investigation shall fill us with shame, He is waiting, waiting, patiently waiting, and will take us if we surrender to Him for service which the red blood of sacrifice colors. We shall become men and women worthwhile to Him, men and women that hasten the building of the city of God and the ending of the battle of the ages.

The Importunate Widow

Charles Haddon Spurgeon (1834–1892) is undoubtedly the most famous minister of the nineteenth century. Converted in 1850, he united with the Baptists and soon began to preach in various places. He became pastor of the Baptist church in Waterbeach, England, in 1851, and three years later he was called to the decaying Park Street Church, London. Within a short time the work began to prosper, a new church was built and dedicated in 1861, and Spurgeon became London's most popular preacher. In 1855, he began to publish his sermons weekly; today they make up the fifty-seven volumes of *The Metropolitan Tabernacle Pulpit*. He founded a pastor's college and several orphanages.

This sermon is taken from *The Metropolitan Tabernacle Pulpit*, volume 15.

Charles Haddon Spurgeon

7

THE IMPORTUNATE WIDOW

Luke 18:1–8

REMEMBER THAT OUR Lord did not only inculcate prayer with great earnestness, but He was Himself a brilliant example of it. It always gives force to a teacher's words when his hearers well know that he carries out his own instructions. Jesus was a prophet mighty both in deed and in word. We read of Him, "Jesus began both to do and to teach." In the exercise of prayer, "cold mountains and the midnight air" witnessed that He was as great a doer as a teacher. When He exhorted His disciples to continue in prayer, and to "pray without ceasing," He only bade them follow in His steps. If any one of all the members of the mystical body might have been supposed to need no prayer, it would certainly have been our Covenant Head; but if our Head abounded in supplication, much more ought we, the inferior members. He was never defiled with the sins which have debased and weakened us spiritually; He had no inbred lusts to struggle with. But if the perfectly pure drew near so often to God, how much more incessant in supplication ought we to be! So mighty, so great, and yet so prayerful! O you weak ones of the flock, how forcibly does the lesson come home to you! Imagine, therefore, the discourse of this morning is not preached to you by me, but comes fresh from the lips of one who was the great master of secret prayer, the highest paragon and pattern of private supplication, and let every word have the force about it as coming from such a One.

Turn we at once to our text, and in it we shall notice, first, *the end and design of the parable*; secondly, we shall have some words to say upon *the two actors in it,* whose characters are intentionally so described as to give force to the reasoning; and then, thirdly, we shall dwell upon *the power which the parable represented as triumphant.*

Our Lord's Design in This Parable

"Men ought always to pray, and not to faint." But can men pray always? There was a sect in the earlier days of Christianity who were foolish enough to read the passage literally and to attempt praying without ceasing by continual repetition of prayers. They of course separated themselves from all worldly concerns, and in order to fulfill one duty of life neglected every other. Such madmen might well expect to reap the due reward of their follies. Happily there is no need in this age for us to reprobate such an error. There is far more necessity to cry out against those who, under the pretense of praying always, have no settled time for prayer at all, and so run to the opposite extreme. Our Lord meant by saying men ought always to pray, that *they ought to be always in the spirit of prayer,* always ready to pray. Like the old knights, always in warfare, not always on their steeds dashing forward with their lances in rest to unhorse an adversary, but always wearing their weapons where they could readily reach them, and always ready to encounter wounds or death for the sake of the cause which they championed. Those grim warriors often slept in their armor; so even when we sleep, we are still to be in the spirit of prayer, so that if perchance we wake in the night we may still be with God.

Our souls, having received the divine centripetal influence which makes it seek its heavenly center, should be evermore naturally rising toward God Himself. Our hearts are to be like those beacons and watchtowers which were prepared along the coast of England when the invasion of the Armada was hourly expected, not always blazing, but with the wood always dry, and the match always there, the whole pile being ready to blaze up at the appointed moment. Our souls should be in such a condition that spontaneous prayer should be very frequent with us. No need to pause in business and leave the counter and fall down upon the knees; the spirit should send up its silent, short, swift petitions to the throne of grace.

When Nehemiah would ask a favor of the king, you will remember that he found an opportunity to do so through the king's asking him, "Why art thou sad?" But before he made him an answer he said, "I prayed unto the King of heaven." Instinctively perceiving the occasion, he did not leap forward to embrace it, but he halted just a moment to ask that he might be enabled to embrace it wisely and fulfill his great design therein. So you and I should often feel, "I cannot do this until I have asked a blessing on it." However impulsively I may spring forward to gain an advantage, yet my spirit, under the influence of divine grace, should hesitate until it has said, "If thy Spirit go not with me, carry me not up hence." A Christian should carry the weapon of all-prayer like a drawn sword in his hand. We should never sheathe our supplications. Never may our hearts be like an unlimbered gun with everything to be done to it before it can thunder on the foe, but it should be like a piece of cannon, loaded and primed, only requiring the fire that it may be discharged. The soul should be not always in the exercise of prayer, but always in the energy of prayer; not always actually praying, but always intentionally praying.

Further, when our Lord says men ought always to pray, He may also have meant that *the whole life of the Christian should be a life of devotion to God.*

> Prayer and praise, with sins forgiven,
> Bring down to earth the bliss of heaven.

To praise God for mercies received both with our voices and with our actions, and then to pray to God for the mercies that we need, devoutly acknowledging that they come from Him, these two exercises in one form or other should make up the sum total of human life. Our life psalm should be composed of alternating verses of praying and of praising until we get into the next world, where the prayer may cease, and praise may swallow up the whole of our immortality. "But," says one, "we have our daily business to attend to." I know you have, but there is a way of making business a part of praise and prayer. You say, "Give us this day our daily bread," and that is a prayer as you utter it; you go off to your work, and as you toil, if you do so in a devout spirit, you are actively praying the same prayer by your lawful labor. You praise God for the mercies received in your morning hymn; and when you go into the duties of life, and there exhibit those graces which reflect honor upon God's name, you are continuing your praises in the best manner. Remember that with Christians to labor is to pray, and that there is much truth in the verse of Coleridge—

He prayeth best who loveth best.

To desire my fellow creatures' good and to seek after it, to desire God's glory, and so to live as to promote it, is the truest of devotion. The devotion of the cloisters is by no means equal to that of the man who is engaged in the battle of life. The devotion of the nunnery and the monastery is at best the heroism of a soldier who shuns the battle. But the devotion of the man in business life, who turns all to the glory of God, is the courage of one who seeks the thickest of the fray, and there bears aloft the grand old standard of Jehovah-nissi. You need not be afraid that there is anything in any lawful calling that need make you desist from vital prayer; but, oh! if your calling is such that you cannot pray in it, you had better leave it. If it be a sinful calling, an unholy calling, of course, you cannot present that to God, but any of the ordinary avocations of life are such that if you cannot sanctify them, it is a want of sanctity in yourself, and the fault lies with you.

Christians ought *always* to pray. It means that when they are using the lapstone or the chisel, when the hands are on the plow handles or on the spade, when they are measuring out the goods, when they are dealing in stocks, whatever they are doing, they are to turn all these things into a part of the sacred pursuit of God's glory. Their common garments are to be vestments, their meals are to be sacraments, their ordinary actions are to be sacrifices, and they themselves a royal priesthood, a peculiar people zealous for good works.

A third meaning which I think our Lord intended to convey to us was that Christians ought always to pray, that is, *they should persevere in prayer.* This is probably His first meaning. When we ask God for a mercy once, we are not to consider that now we are not further to trouble Him with it, but we are to come to Him again and again. If we have asked of Him seven times, we ought to continue until seventy times seven. In temporal mercies there may be a limit, and the Holy Spirit may bid us ask no more. Then must we say, the "Lord's will be done." If it be anything for our own personal advantage, we must let the Spirit of submission rule us, so that after having sought the Lord thrice, we shall be content with the promise, "My grace is sufficient for thee," and no longer ask that the thorn in the flesh should be removed.

But in spiritual mercies, and especially in the united prayers of a church, there is no taking a denial. Here, if we would prevail, we must persist. We must continue incessantly and constantly, and know no pause to our prayer until we win the mercy to the fullest possible extent. "Men ought always to pray." Week by week, month by month, year by year, the conversion of that dear child is to be the parents' main plea. The bringing in of that unconverted husband is to lie upon the wife's heart night and day until she gets it. She is not to take even ten or twenty years of unsuccessful prayer as a reason why she should cease. She is to set God no times nor seasons, but so long as there is life in her and life in the dear object of her solicitude, she is to continue still to plead with the mighty God of Jacob. The pastor is not to seek a blessing on his people occasionally, and then in receiving a measure of it to desist from further intercession; but he is to continue vehemently without pause, without restraining his energies, to cry aloud and spare not until the windows of heaven be opened and a blessing be given too large for him to house.

But, brethren, how many times we ask of God and have not because we do not wait long enough at the door! We knock a time or two at the gate of mercy, and as no friendly messenger opens the door, we go our ways. Too many prayers are like boys' runaway knocks, given, and then the giver is away before the door can be opened. O for grace to stand foot to foot with the angel of God, and never, never, never relax our hold; feeling that the cause we plead is one in which we must be successful, for souls depend on it, the glory of God is connected with it, the state of our fellow men is in jeopardy. If we could have given up in prayer our own lives and the lives of those dearest to us, yet the souls of men we cannot give up; we must urge and plead again and again until we obtain the answer.

> The humble suppliant cannot fail
> To have his wants supplied,
> Since he for sinners intercedes
> Who once for sinners died.

I cannot leave this part of the subject without observing that our Lord would have us learn that *believers should be more frequent in prayer*. Not only should they always have the spirit of prayer and make their whole lives a prayer and persevere in any one object which is dear to their souls, but there should be a greater frequency of prayer amongst all the saints. I gather that from the parable, "lest by her continual coming she weary me." Prayerfulness will scarcely be kept up long unless you set apart times and seasons for prayer. There are no times laid down in Scripture except by the example of holy men, for the Lord trusts much to the love of His people and to the spontaneous motions of the inner life. He does not say, "Pray at seven o'clock in the morning every day," or "pray at night at eight, or nine, or ten, or eleven" but says, "Pray without ceasing." Yet every Christian will find it exceedingly useful to have his regular times for retirement, and I doubt whether any eminent piety can be maintained without these seasons being very carefully and scrupulously observed. We read in the old traditions of James the apostle that he prayed so much that his knees grew hard through his long kneeling. It is recorded by Fox that Latimer, during the time of his imprisonment, was so much upon his knees that frequently the poor old man could not rise to his meals and had to be lifted up by his servants. When he could no longer preach and was immured within stone walls, his prayers went up to heaven for his country, and we in these times are receiving the blessing. Daniel prayed with his windows open daily and at regular intervals. "Seven times a day," says one, "will I praise thee." David declared that at "Evening, and morning, and at noon," would he wait upon God. O that our intervals of prayer were not so distant one from the other; would God that on the pilgrimage of life the wells at which we drink were more frequent. In this way should we continue in prayer.

Our Lord means, to sum up the whole, that *believers should exercise a universality of supplication*—we ought to pray at all times. There are no canonical hours in the Christian's day or week. We should pray from cock-crowing to midnight, at such times as the Spirit moves us. We should pray in all estates, in our poverty and in our wealth, in our health and in our sickness, in the bright days of festival and in the dark nights of lamentation. We should pray at the birth and pray at the funeral, we should pray when our soul is glad within us by reason of abundant mercy, and we should pray when our soul draws nigh to the rates of death by reason of heaviness. We should pray in all transactions, whether secular or religious. Prayer should sanctify everything. The Word of God and prayer should come in over and above the common things of daily life. Pray over a bargain, pray over going into the shop and coming out again. Remember in the days of Joshua how the Gibeonites deceived Israel because Israel inquired not of the Lord, and be not deceived yourself by a specious temptation, as you may well be if you do not daily come to the Lord, and say, "Guide me: make straight a plain path for my feet, and lead me in the way everlasting." You shall never err by praying too much. You shall never make a mistake by asking God's guidance too often. But you shall find this to be the gracious illumination of your eyes, if in the turning of the road where two paths meet which seem to be equally right, you shall stay a moment and cry to God, "Guide me, O thou great Jehovah." "Men ought always to pray." I have enlarged upon it from this pulpit, go you and expound it in your daily lives.

Two Actors

In enforcing this precept, our Lord gives us a parable in which there are two actors, the characteristics of the two actors being such as to add strength to His precept.

In the first verse of the parable there is *a judge*. Now, herein is the great advantage to us in prayer. Brethren, if this poor woman prevailed with a judge whose office is stern, unbending, untender, how much more ought you and I to be instant in prayer and hopeful of success when we have to supplicate a Father! Far other is a father than a judge. The judge must necessarily be impartial, stern, but the father is necessarily partial to his child, compassionate and tender to his own offspring. Does she prevail over a judge and shall not we prevail with our Father who is in heaven? And does she continue in her desperate need to weary him until she wins what she desires. Shall we not continue in the agony of our desires until we get from our heavenly Father whatsoever His Word has promised?

In addition to being a judge, he was *devoid of all good character*. In both branches he failed. He "feared not God." Conscience was seared in him, he had no thoughts of the great judgment seat before which judges must appear. Though possibly he had taken an oath before God to judge impartially, yet he forgot his oath and trod justice under his foot. "Neither did he regard man." The approbation of his fellow creatures, which is very often a power, even with naturally bad men, either to restrain them from overt evil or else to constrain them to righteousness, this principle had no effect upon him. Now, if the widow prevailed over such a wretch as this, if the iron of her importunity broke the iron and steel of this man's obduracy, how much more may we expect to be successful with Him who is righteous, and just, and good, the Friend of the needy, the Father of the fatherless, and the Avenger of all such as are oppressed! O let the character of God as it rises before you in all its majesty of truthfulness and faithfulness blended with lovingkindness, and tenderness, and mercy, excite in you an indefatigable ardor of supplication, making you resolve with this poor woman that you will never cease to supplicate until you win your suit.

The judge was a man so unutterably bad that he *even confessed his badness to himself*, with great contentment too. Without the slightest tinge of remorse, he said within himself, "Though I fear not God, neither regard man." There are few sinners who will go to this length. They may neither fear God nor regard men, yet still they will indulge in their minds some semblance of that which is virtuous and cheat themselves into the belief that at least they are not worse than others. But with this man there was no self-deception. He was as cool about this avowal as the Pharisee was concerning the opposite, "God, I thank thee that I am not as other men are." To what a brazen impertinence must this man have come, to what an extent must he have hardened his mind, that knowing himself to be such, he yet climbed the judgment seat and sat there to judge his fellow men! Yet the woman prevailed with this monster in human form, who had come to take pleasure in his own wickedness and gloated in the badness of his own heart. Over this man importunity prevailed—how much more over him who spared not his own Son, but freely delivered Him up for us all; how much more over Him whose name is love, whose nature is everything that is attractive and encouraging to such as seek His face! The worse this judge appears, and he could scarcely have been painted in blacker colors, the more does the voice of the Savior seem to say to us, "Men ought always to pray, and not to faint."

Note with regard to the character of this judge that

he was one who *consciously cared for nothing but his own ease.* When at last he consented to do justice, the only motive which moved him was, "lest by her continual coming she weary me." "She *stun* me," might be the Greek word—a kind of slang, I suppose, of that period, meaning lest "she batter me," "she bruise me," and as some translate it, "black my fate with her incessant constant batterings." That was the kind of language he used; a short quick sentence of indignation at being bothered, as we should say, by such a case as this. The only thing that moved him was a desire to be at ease and to take things comfortably. O brethren, if she could prevail over such a one, how much more shall we speed with God whose delight it is to take care of His children who loves them even as the apple of His eye!

This judge was *practically unkind and cruel* to her; yet the widow continued. For awhile he would not listen to her, though her household, her life, her children's comfort, were all hanging upon his will, he left her by a passive injustice to suffer still. But our God has been practically kind and gracious to us, up to this moment He has heard us and granted our requests. Set this against the character of the judge, and surely every loving heart that knows the power of prayer will be moved to incessant importunity.

We must, however, pass on now to notice the other actor in the scene—the widow; and here everything tells again the same way, to induce the church of God to be importunate. She was apparently *a perfect stranger to the judge.* She appeared before him as an individual in whom he took no interest. He had possibly never seen her before; who she was and what she wanted was no concern to him. But when the church appears before God she comes as Christ's own bride, she appears before the Father as one whom He has loved with an everlasting love. And shall He not avenge His own elect, His own chosen, His own people? Shall not their prayers prevail with Him when a stranger's importunity won a suit of an unwilling judge?

The widow appeared at the judgment seat *without a*

friend. According to the parable, she had no advocate, no powerful pleader to stand up in the court and say, "I am the patron of this humble woman." If she prevailed, she must prevail by her own ardor and her own intensity of purpose. But when you and I come before our Father, we come not alone, for—

> He is at the Father's side,
> The Man of love, the Crucified.

We have a Friend who ever lives to make intercession for us. O Christian, urge your suit with holy boldness, press your ease, for the blood of Jesus speaks with a voice that must be heard. Be not therefore faint in your spirit, but continue instant in your supplication.

This poor woman came *without a promise to encourage her,* no, with the reverse, with much to discourage. But when you and I come before God, we are commanded to pray by God Himself. We are promised that if we ask it shall be given us, if we seek we shall find. Does she win without the sacred weapon of the promise, and shall not we win who can set the battering-rams of God's own word against the gates of heaven, a battering-ram that shall make every timber in those gates to quiver? O brethren, we must not pause nor cease a moment while we have God's promise to back our plea.

The widow, in addition to having no promise whatever, was even *without the right of constant access.* She had, I suppose, a right to clamor to be heard at ordinary times when judgment was administered, but what right had she to dog the judge's footsteps, to waylay him in the streets, to hammer at his private door, to be heard calling at nightfall, so that he, sleeping at the top of his house, was awakened by her cries? She had no permission so to importune, but we may come to God at all times and all seasons. We may cry day and night to Him, for He has bidden us pray without ceasing. What, without a permit is this woman so incessant! And with the sacred permissions which God has given us, and the encouragement of abounding lovingkindness, shall we cease to plead?

soul, every time she prayed, *provoked the*
of anger were on his face. I doubt not he
e mouth to think he should be wearied by
a person so insignificant. But with Jesus, every time
we plead we please Him rather than provoke Him. The
prayers of the saints are the music of God's ears.

> To him there's music in a groan,
> And beauty in a tear.

We, speaking after the manner of men, bring a
gratification to God when we intercede with Him. He
is vexed with us if we restrain our supplications; He is
pleased with us when we draw near constantly. Oh,
then, as you see the smile upon the Father's face,
children of His love, I beseech you faint not, but
continue still without ceasing to entreat the blessing.

Once more, this woman had a suit in which *the judge
could not be himself personally interested.* But ours is a
case in which the God we plead with is more interested
than we are; for when a church asks for the conversion
of souls, she may justly say, "Arise, O God, plead thine
own cause." It is for the honor of Christ that souls should
be converted. It brings glory to the mercy and power of
God when great sinners are turned from the error of
their ways. Consequently, we are pleading for the Judge
with the Judge, for God we are pleading with God. Our
prayer is virtually *for* Christ as *through* Christ that His
kingdom may come and His will may be done.

I must not forget to mention that in this woman's
case *she was only one.* She prevailed though she was
only one, but shall not God avenge His own elect who
are not one but tens of thousands? If there be a promise that if two or three are agreed it shall be done, how
much more if in any church hundreds meet together
with unanimous souls anxiously desiring that God
would fulfill His promise? These pleas cast chains
around the throne of God! How do they, as it were,
hem in omnipotence! How they constrain the Almighty
to arise out of His place and come in answer to His
people, and do the great deed which shall bless His
church and glorify Himself.

You see, then, whether we consider the judge or consider the widow, each character has points about it which tend to make us see our duty and our privilege to pray without ceasing.

The Power That Triumphed

This power was not the woman's eloquence, "I pray thee avenge me of mine adversary." These words are very few. They have the merit of being very expressive, but he that would study oratory will not gather many lessons from them. "I pray thee avenge me of mine adversary." Just eight words. You observe there is no plea, there is nothing about her widowhood, nothing urged about her children, nothing said about the wickedness of her adversary, nothing concerning the judgment of God upon unjust judges, nor about the wrath of God upon unjust men who devour widows' houses—nothing of the kind. "I pray thee avenge me of mine adversary." Her success, therefore, did not depend upon her power in rhetoric, and we learn from this that the prevalence of a soul or of a church with God does not rest upon the elocution of its words or upon the eloquence of its language. The prayer which mounts to heaven may have but very few of the tail feathers of adornment about it, but it must have the strong wing feathers of intense desire. It must not be as the peacock, gorgeous for beauty, but it must be as the eagle, for soaring aloft, if it would ascend up to the seventh heavens. When you pray in public, as a rule, the shorter the better. Words are cumbersome to prayer. It often happens that an abundance of words reveals a scarcity of desires. Verbiage is generally nothing better in prayer than a miserable fig leaf with which to cover the nakedness of an unawakened soul.

Another thing is quite certain, namely, that the woman *did not prevail through the merits of her case.* It may have been a very good case; there is nothing said about that. I do not doubt the rightness of it. But still, the judge did not know nor care whether it was right or wrong; all he cared about was that this woman troubled him. He does not say, "She has a good case, and I ought to listen to it." No, he was too bad a man to be moved by such a motive—but "she worries me," that is all, "I will attend to it." So in our suit—in the suit of a sinner with God—it is not the merit of his case that can ever prevail with God. You have no merit. If you are to win, another's merit must stand instead of yours, and on your part it must not be merit but misery; it must not be your righteousness but your importunity that is to prevail with God. How this ought to encourage those of you who are laboring under a sense of unworthiness! However unworthy you may be, continue in prayer. Black may be the hand, but if it can but lift the knocker, the gate will open. Aye, though you have a palsy in that hand; though, in addition to that palsy, you be leprous and the white leprosy be on your forehead, yet if you cannot but tremblingly lift up that knocker and let it fall by its own weight upon that sacred promise, you shall surely get an audience with the King of Kings. It is not eloquence, it is not merit that wins with God, it is nothing but importunity.

Note with regard to this woman that the judge said first, she troubled him; next he said, she came continually; then he added his fear, lest "she weary me." I think the case was somewhat after this fashion. The judge was sitting one morning on his bench and many were the persons coming before him asking justice, which he was dealing out with the impartiality of a villain, giving always his best word to him who brought the heaviest bribes; when presently a poor woman uttered her plaint. She had tried to be heard several times, but her voice had been drowned by others. But this time it was more shrill and sharp, and she caught the judge's eye. "My lord, avenge me of mine adversary." He no sooner sees from her poverty-stricken dress that there are no bribes to be had, than he replies, "Hold your tongue! I have other business to attend to." He goes on with another suit in which the fees were more attractive. Still he hears the cry again, "My lord, I am a widow, avenge me of mine adversary." Vexed with the renewed disturbance, he bade the usher put her out because she interrupted the silence of the court and stopped the public business. "Take care she does not get in again tomorrow," said he. "She is a troublesome woman." Long before the morrow had come, he found out the truth of his opinion. She waited until he left the court, dogged his footsteps, and followed him through the streets, until he was glad to get through his door. He bade the servants fasten it lest that noisy widow should come in, for she had constantly assailed him with the cry, "Avenge me of mine adversary." He is now safely within doors and bids the servants bring in his meal. They are pouring water on his hands and feet, his lordship is about to enjoy his repast, when a heavy knock is heard at the door, followed by a clamor, pushing, and a scuffle. "What is it?" says he. "It is a woman outside, a widow woman, who wants your lordship to see justice done her." "Tell her I cannot attend to her. She must be gone." He seeks his rest at nightfall on the housetop when he hears a heavy knock at the door, and a voice comes up from the street beneath his residence, "My lord, avenge me of mine adversary." The next morning his court is open, and, though she is forbidden to enter, like a dog that will enter somehow, she finds her way in and interrupts the court continually with her plea, "My lord, avenge me of mine adversary."

Ask her why she is thus importunate, and she will tell you her husband is dead, and he left a little plot of land. It was all they had, and a cruel neighbor who looked with greedy eyes upon that little plot has taken it as Ahab took Naboth's vineyard. Now she is without any meal or any oil for the little ones, and they are crying for food. Oh, if their father had been alive, how he would have guarded their interests! But she has no helper, and the case is a glaring one. What is a judge for if he is not to protect the injured? She has no other chance, for the creditor is about to take away her children to sell them into bondage. She cannot bear that. "No," she says, "I have but one chance. It is that this man should speak up for me and do me justice. I have

made up my mind he shall never rest until he does so.
I am resolved that if I perish, the last words on my lips
shall be, 'Avenge me of mine adversary.'"

So the court is continually interrupted. Again the
judge shouts, "Put her out; put her out! I cannot conduct the business at all with this crazy woman here
continually dinning in my ears a shriek of 'Avenge me
of mine adversary.'" But it is sooner said than done,
she lays hold of the pillars of the court so as not to be
dragged out. When at last they get her in the street,
she does but wait her chance to enter again. She pur-
sues the judge along the highways; she never lets him
have a minute's peace. "Well," says the judge, "I am
worried out of my very life. I care not for the widow,
nor her property, nor her children. Let them starve;
what are they to me? But I cannot stand this, it will
weary me beyond measure. I will see to it." It is done,
and she goes her way. Nothing but her importunity
prevails.

Now, brethren, you have many other weapons to use
with God in prayer, but our Savior bids you not neglect
this master, all-conquering instrument of importunity.
God will be more easily moved than this unjust judge,
only be you as importunate as this widow was. If you
are sure it is a right thing for which you are asking,
plead now, plead at noon, plead at night, plead on.
With cries and tears spread out your case, order your
arguments, back up your pleas with reasons, urge the
precious blood of Jesus, set the wounds of Christ before the Father's eyes, bring out the atoning sacrifice,
point to Calvary, enlist the crowned Prince, the Priest
who stands at the right hand of God. Resolve in your
very soul that if Zion does not flourish, if souls be not
saved, if your family be not blessed, if your own zeal be
not revived, yet you will die with the plea upon your
lips and with the importunate wish upon your spirits.
Let me tell you that if any of you should die with your
prayers unanswered, you need not conclude that God
has disappointed you.

With one story I will finish. I have heard that a

certain godly father had the unhappiness to be the parent of some five or six most graceless sons. All of them as they grew up imbibed infidel sentiments and led a libidinous life. The father, who had been constantly praying for them and was a pattern of every virtue, hoped at least that in his death he might be able to say a word that should move their hearts. He gathered them to his bedside, but his unhappiness in dying was extreme, for he lost the light of God's countenance, and was beset with doubts and fears. The last black thought that haunted him was, "Instead of my death being a testimony for God, which will win my dear sons, I die in such darkness and gloom that I fear I shall confirm them in their infidelity and lead them to think that there is nothing in Christianity at all." The effect was the reverse.

The sons came around the grave at the funeral, and when they returned to the house, the eldest son thus addressed his brothers: "My brothers, throughout his lifetime our father often spoke to us about religion. We have always despised it, but what a sermon his death-bed has been to us! For if he who served God so well and lived so near to God found it so hard a thing to die, what kind of death may we expect ours to be who have lived without God and without hope?" The same feeling possessed them all, and thus the father's death had strangely answered the prayers of his life through the grace of God.

You cannot tell but what, when you are in glory, you should look down from the windows of heaven and receive a double heaven in beholding your dear sons and daughters converted by the words you left behind. I do not say this to make you cease pleading for their immediate conversion, but to encourage you. Never give up prayer, never be tempted to cease from it. So long as there is breath in your body, and breath in their bodies, continue still to pray, for I tell you that He will avenge you speedily though He bear long with you. God bless these words for Jesus' sake. Amen.

The Ten Virgins

Robert Murray McCheyne (1813–1843) is one of the brightest lights of the Church of Scotland. Born in Dundee, he was educated in Edinburgh and licensed to preach in 1835. For a brief time, he assisted his friend Andrew A. Bonar at Larbert and Dunipace. In 1836 he was ordained and installed as pastor of Saint Peter's Church, Dundee, where he served until his untimely death two months short of his thirtieth birthday. He was known for his personal sanctity and his penetrating ministry of the Word, and great crowds came to hear him preach. *The Memoirs of and Remains of Robert Murray McCheyne* by Andrew Bonar is a Christian classic that every minister of the gospel should read.

This series of four brief messages is taken from *The Additional Remains of Rev. R. M. McCheyne*, published in 1846 in Edinburgh by William Oliphant and Co.

Robert Murray McCheyne

8

THE TEN VIRGINS

Matthew 25:1–13

THERE IS NOT in the whole Bible a parable that applies more accurately to this congregation than this. Like the ten virgins, you may all be divided into two classes. Some of you are wise, I trust; and some, alas! are foolish. Like the virgins, you all profess a great deal; yet some have the gift of the Holy Spirit, and some want it. And the day is fast hastening when you will be separated. The truly saved among you will enter in with Christ; the rest will be shut out for eternity. At present I can overtake only three facts.

PART 1

God's Children Are Wise; The Rest Are Foolish

Those of you who are God's children are truly wise. *First*, not worldly wise. This is denied: "Ye see your calling, brethren, how that not many wise men after the flesh, not many mighty, not many noble are called: but God hath chosen the foolish things of the world to confound the wise" (1 Cor. 1:26–27). And "the wisdom of this world is foolishness with God" (1 Cor. 3:19). "I thank thee, O Father, Lord of heaven and earth, because thou hast hid these things from the wise and prudent, and hast revealed them unto babes" (Matt. 11:25). "Out of the mouth of babes and sucklings hast thou ordained strength" (Ps. 8:2). Not many of deep, profound mind are saved, not many men of learning, not many of your sagacious, worldly men, men wise to drive a bargain. These are often passed by; and God takes some little child that knows nothing of the world, or some peasant from behind his plow, and brings him to glory. Why? Just that no man may boast and say: It was my wit that saved me. *Second,* yet God's children are wise—the only wise in this world.

1. *They see things as they truly are.* You that are mere professors do not see things as they truly are. (a) You do not see *time* as it truly is—the threshold of eternity. You do not see how short it is—that three score and ten years are but a span. You do not see how rapidly it passes—like the swift ship—like the eagle to the prey. You do not see that it cannot be recalled, and that every moment is precious—that it is the time for conversion—the only time; else you could not waste it in mere pretenses to godliness. They that are Christ's see time as it really is. (b) You do not see *yourselves* as you truly are. You have never seen what it is to be by nature children of wrath. You have never seen the awful mountains of sin that are piled over your soul. You have never seen the lusts that bind your soul—the deep volcano of burning lust that is in your own bosom. They that are Christ's see this somewhat as it truly is. (c) You do not see *the favor of God.* You have never seen how precious it is. You know the value of the favor of man, and therefore you wear a cloak of profession; but you know not the value of God's favor, or you would fly to Christ. They that are Christ's know this as it is.

2. *God's children do not rest in knowledge.* Hypocrites always rest in their knowledge. You never can tell them anything new. They say: I know that. Tell them of sin, of Christ, of judgment to come—they think they shall be saved because they have knowledge; although this knowledge has never led them to rest on Christ, to pray, to leave their sins. But you that are Christ's do not rest content with this. You not only know of Christ and speak of Him, but you do the things that He says. You have turned from idols. You are the only wise.

3. *A child of God lives for eternity.* A hypocrite lives for time. This was all Judas lived for—if he could pass off for a while as a true disciple—if he could keep up

appearances for a time—if he could indulge his lusts, and yet be esteemed a believer and a true apostle. He tried to keep up appearances to the last. So Demas wanted to deceive Paul for this life—to be thought a brother. Alas, how many of you are thus foolish—living so as to keep up an appearance of being a Christian for a little time, though you know that you are living in positive sin, and that you will be discovered before the world in a short time. You only are truly wise who live for eternity—who live as you shall wish you had done when you come to die.

4. *A child of God is like God.* God is the only wise. In Him are all the fountains of divine wisdom. God is light and in Him is no darkness at all. To become like Him is to become truly wise. Those of you who have fled to Christ are becoming like God. You have got His Spirit, and you are being changed into His image. You have one will with God. You fall in with God's purposes in this world. His joy is your joy. You that are mere professors have none of God's likeness. You do not seek it, nor desire it.

The Wise and Foolish Are Alike in Many Things

The virgins were alike in many things. To the eye of man they appeared the same. All were virgins, dressed probably in white—all their faces probably fair and comely. Each of the ten carried a silver lamp, bright and polished, and every lamp was lighted. No, all of them seemed to have one object in view. They went forth to meet the bridegroom. In one thing alone they differed. The foolish took no oil in their lamps; but the wise took oil in their vessels with their lamps. So it is with professors and God's children to this day.

In many things man can see no difference.

1. *You enjoy the same ordinances.* (a) You sit under the same pastor—in the same seats. You come up together to the house of God in company. (b) You sing the same psalms. Your voices blend together, and no ear but that of God can distinguish the voice of the hypocrite from that of the wise virgin. (c) You stand up

at the same prayer—all equally reverent in appearance. (d) You listen to the same sermons. Sometimes you will be affected together. The feeling of sympathy runs through the midst of you, and none can tell where it is like early dew, or where it is the dew of the Spirit— the sympathy of nature or the sympathy of grace. (e) You sit down at the same Lord's table and pass the bread from hand to hand—you pass the cup from one to another. Ah! How affecting it is to think that so many in this congregation are but foolish virgins—that you will be parted in eternity.

2. *They use the same speech.* God's children speak the language of Canaan; but professors learn to imitate it, and at last no one can discover the difference. They speak of convictions of sin, awakening, getting light, seeking Christ, finding Christ, closing with Christ, finding peace—when all the time their hearts are far from God, and they are lovers of pleasure more than lovers of God. Oh, how sad it is to think that many a tongue that has spoken much about Christ and regeneration and the Holy Spirit shall yet want a drop of water to cool it in the burning lake.

3. *They utter the same prayers.* One of the great marks of a child of God is prayer. He loves to pray: "Behold, he prayeth." But even this is imitated by professors who have a name to live and are dead. Often they will pray in secret with great meltings and affections; often they will pray in public with great fervor and pathos; yet all the time they are living in sin and know it. Alas! How sad, that many of you whose voices have often been heard in prayer may yet be heard crying, "Lord, Lord, open to us"—crying on rocks and mountains to cover you from the wrath of God and of the Lamb!

4. *They have the same outward behavior.* The truest mark of children of God is their avoiding sin. They flee from their old companions and old ways—they walk with God; yet even this is imitated by the foolish virgins. They go out to meet their Lord. They flee old sins for a time. They hasten from their work to the house of God.

They seek the company of God's children—perhaps they try to save others and become very zealous in this. O how sad that many who now cling to the godly will soon be torn from them and bound up with devils and wicked men!

An Important Difference

There is an important difference between the foolish and the wise. The foolish virgins have no oil in their vessels. Professors are often striven with by the Spirit. In the days of Noah he strove long to get men to leave their sins and enter the ark (see Gen. 6:3). So also with Israel in the wilderness: "They rebelled, and vexed his holy spirit" (Isa. 63:10). And even in the days of Stephen: "Ye do always resist the Holy Ghost: as your fathers did, so do ye" (Acts 7:51). In the Bible, in the ministry—by mercies, by afflictions—He strives like a man wrestling with you. He strives to make you quit your sins and flee into Christ. Most of you have, in each or all of these ways, felt the Spirit's strivings.

1. *They are not taught by the Spirit.* All who are saved are taught by the Spirit—"all taught of God." Without this, no man will come to Christ, for the soul is dead. He teaches our lost condition, then He glorifies Christ. 11|2|2015

2. *They are not dwelt in by the Spirit.* The Spirit dwells in all who come to Christ (John 7:37). (a) As a seal: "In whom also after that ye believed, ye were sealed" (Eph. 1:13). The heart is the wax—the Holy Spirit the seal—the image of Christ the impression. He softens the heart and presses on the seal; but not like other seals—He does not lift it away, but keeps it there. (b) As a witness: "The Spirit itself beareth witness with our spirit" (Rom. 8:16). The spirit of adoption, crying "Abba" in the heart, is the Spirit bearing witness. When the soul is taken into the child's place, it can use a child's liberty. (c) As an earnest: "The earnest of the Spirit in our hearts" (2 Cor. 1:22). A little in hand of the full reward. The Holy Spirit in the heart is a little of heaven—the peace, joy, holy breathings, humility,

communion of heaven, all begun. Ah, my friends! Be not deceived. Do not tell me you sit under this or that minister, have had those convictions, liberty in prayer, but are you changed? Have you gotten the new heart—is heaven begun? Have you oil in your vessels with your lamps?

PART 2

The Tarrying of the Bridegroom

In that memorable discourse of the Savior with His disciples on the night of the last supper, Jesus said to them: "A little while, and ye shall not see me: and again, a little while, and ye shall see me, because I go to the Father" (John 16:16). And again, John, in the Revelation, heard Him say: "Behold, I come as a thief. Blessed is he that watcheth, and keepeth his garments, lest he walk naked, and they see his shame." And His last word, which fell like heavenliest music on John's enraptured ear, was: "Behold, I come quickly," and, "Surely, I come quickly." Many of the first Christians seem to have thought that He would come in their day. So that Paul, in Second Thessalonians, had to warn them that the great Romish apostasy must happen first. And we find that scoffers in Peter's time used to say: "Where is the promise of His coming?" Century after century has rolled away since then, and yet Jesus has never come. This explains the word, "The bridegroom tarried." Certainly He desires to come: "His desire is toward me." It will be the day of the gladness of His heart—the bridal day. And those that love Christ love His appearing. They cry, like John, "Even so, come, Lord Jesus." Yet still He tarries. Why is this?

1. *He is not willing that any should perish.* "The Lord is not slack concerning his promise, as some men count slackness; but is longsuffering to us-ward, not willing that any should perish, but that all should come to repentance" (2 Peter 3:9). This is the reason why He tarries: He is slow to anger. Sometimes, when I see some act of gross and open wickedness, my heart

trembles within me. Then I think how the Lord sees all this—aye, all the wickedness committed over the whole world—and yet He forbears. Ah, what a sight of forbearance and long-suffering compassion is here! This is the reason why He tarries: He has compassion for the vilest and waits long before He comes.

2. *To fill up the number of His elect.* Christ is at this moment gathering a people from among the Gentiles. He is building up the great temple of the Lord, adding stone to stone. He cannot come until this is done. When all this is done, then He will come and put on the top-stone with shoutings of "Grace, grace unto it." He told Paul to remain and preach at Corinth: "For I have much people in this city." For the same reason He makes His ministers remain and preach on; for He has much people still. When He comes, those that are ready will enter in with Him to the marriage and the door will be shut. There are, no doubt, many elect ones, many that were given Him by the Father before the foundation of the world, still in the sleep of nature. He waits until these are gathered. When the last of His elect are gathered, then He will come.

3. *To try the graces of His people.* There are many of the graces of God's people that can only grow in time of affliction. There is a plant in the garden which the gardener tramples below his feet to make it grow better; so it is with many of the graces of God's children—they grow better by being tried. (a) Faith in His Word. The world says: "Where is the promise of His coming? All things continue as they were." All things seen are against it. Can you look through to the unseen world? This is what is wanted: "We look not at the things which are seen, but at the things which are not seen." Now this is one reason why the Bridegroom tarries: that faith may grow. (b) Bear with adversaries. If He came now and avenged us of our adversary, we would have no scope for forgiving injuries or bearing reproaches for His name. We must be conformable to His death; therefore He bears long with us. (c) Compassion for souls. This was the most remarkable

feature in Christ's character. This brought Him from the throne of glory—this made Him weep upon Mount Olivet. It behooves us to be made like Him in this also. But this is the only time when we can be like Him in this: when Jesus comes, we will cry, "Just and true are thy ways, thou King of saints," while He tramples His enemies below His feet. Do not wonder that Jesus tarries.

The Sleep of the Virgins

"They all slumbered and slept." These words have been interpreted several ways. I have no doubt that the simplest interpretation is the true one—that before Christ comes all the Christian churches will fall into a deep slumber. The Bible shows that not only do hypocrites fall asleep, but true believers also. Hence we find the apostles sleeping at the Mount of Transfiguration and again at Gethsemane. Paul cries to the Romans, "It is high time to awake out of sleep."

1. *How Christians sleep.* (a) The eyes begin to shut. When first brought to Christ, the eyes of sinners were opened to see the shortness of time—that it is but a span; the vanity of the world—all vain show; the exceeding sinfulness of sin. They saw sin covering them all over like devils and were amazed that they were out of hell. They saw Christ in all His beauty, fullness, and glory. But now all these things become dim as to a sleeping man. All outward objects are hidden—the soul sees no longer the shortness of time, the emptiness of the world, the vileness of sin, the glory of Christ. (b) The ear does not hear His knockings. Once the ear heard His voice. Amid a thousand the voice of Christ was sweet and powerful. Now the soul hears as if it did not hear: "I have put off my coat; how shall I put it on? I have washed my feet; how shall I defile them?" (c) The sleeper dreams. So the soul takes up with idols— vain fancies. When first awakened, the soul said, "What have I to do any more with idols?" But now when Christ and divine things are hidden, the soul again takes up with vain idols. Hence comes, *first*, deadness in prayer.

How sweet prayer is to a believing soul! There is wonderful access to the throne—pouring out of the heart—no separation—nothing kept back. But now there is utter barrenness—the soul has no desire—no free access. *Second*, a fearful spirit. A sense of guilt now lies on the conscience—a stupefying sense of having offended God—a spirit of bondage. *Third*, the believer does not fear sin. Once a sweet trembling fear of sin—a keeping far from the occasions of it, like Joseph: "How shall I commit this great wickedness?" Now there is a fearful familiarity with sin.

2. *How hypocrites sleep.* (a) They lose all their convictions. At one time they had deep and clear convictions of sin; but now they lose them. They have gone into some open sin and drowned conviction—they quench the Spirit. (b) They lose their joy in divine things. The stony-ground hearers received the Word with joy—a flash of delight. Something about the Word attracts their fancy—eloquence or imagery. Or, hoping they are converted, they flatter themselves and take great delight in hearing. This soon dies away. (c) They give over prayer. For a long time they prayed in a very melting manner. When under convictions, or under illuminations and a false hope, or before others, they prayed with fluency; but now they give over prayer by degrees. "They all slumbered and slept." They have been out in company or they are sleepy or they have no relish for it, and so they give over prayer by degrees.

Between the two there is this great difference that the godly have still oil in their vessels, the others none. I would not say a word to encourage you who are godly to sleep on. On the contrary, it is high time to awake out of sleep. But I cannot but remark how different is the sleep of the two. (a) The godly will waken out of their sleep. It is very sinful and very dangerous, but it is not fatal. The hypocrite seldom ever wakens out of his sleep. The rarest conversion in the world is that of a hardened hypocrite. (b) While the godly are under the displeasure of God, yet they are not under His curse; but the hypocrite sleeps over hell.

The Coming of the Bridegroom

At midnight, at an unexpected time, Christ will come. The whole Bible shows this: "Of that day and hour knoweth no man, no, not the angels of heaven but my Father only." "Watch, therefore; for ye know neither the day nor the hour when the Son of Man cometh." It is compared to lightning: "For as the lightning cometh out of the east, and shineth even unto the west; so shall also the coming of the Son of Man be." What more awfully sudden than lightning! First an awful stillness, the black, inky clouds shrouding the sky—then a bright gleam from east to west. So shall His coming be. It is like travail on a woman with child: "When they shall say, Peace and safety; then sudden destruction cometh upon them as travail upon a woman with child; and they shall not escape." It is like a thief: "The day of the Lord so cometh, as a thief in the night." It is thus in two respects: (a) In the uncertainty of the hour. When a thief is going to break into a house, he does not tell the hour at which he will come. He gives no signs of his approach. If the good man of the house knew what hour he would come, he would sit up and not suffer his house to be broken up. Such will the coming of the Bridegroom be: "Ye know neither the day nor the hour when the Son of Man cometh." (b) A thief comes at the hour of rest. When the family have all gone to rest, when the good man of the house has locked and barred the door, when every candle is put out and every eye is sealed in sleep, then the thief comes and forces the bar and enters in. Such will the coming of the Savior be. When the world is steeped in slumber Jesus will come.

Some of you will say: "Surely we shall have some guess of the time of His coming." Now, if there be one thing plainer than another, it is that you know neither the day nor the hour: "In such an hour as ye think not, the Son of Man cometh." If I were to go around you all and say, "Do you think the Son of Man will come to-night?" you would all say, "I think not." Well, just in such an hour He will come. Are you ready?

A Word to the Unconverted

1. *Some of you live in dishonesty.* In buying and selling some of you, perhaps, use the light weight and the false balance, or in some other way you deceive your neighbor. O how dreadful if Christ should come and find you thus! It is said men will be buying and selling when He comes.

2. *Some live in deeds of darkness.* Perhaps you say, Surely the darkness shall cover me: "At the window of my house I looked through my casement, and beheld among the simple ones, I discerned among the youths, a young man void of understanding, passing through the street near her corner; and he went the way to her house, in the twilight, in the evening, in the black and dark night." Some of you commit those things of which it is a shame even so much as to speak. How awful will it be to you when His holy face appears!

3. *Some of you stifle convictions.* Like Agrippa, you are almost persuaded to be a Christian. Like Felix, you tremble and say, "A more convenient season." Some of you put off your convictions with a little gaiety, a little worldly pleasure, saying, Plenty of time before I die. Ah! what will you do when the cry comes at midnight? No time for a prayer—no time for your Bible then—no time for conversion. "At midnight there was a cry."

PART 3

There is something sweet in that midnight cry, "Behold, the Bridegroom cometh." It will be an awful day even to a child of God. *First*, all sudden changes are dreadful. Many persons have been killed by the sudden news of something joyful. How awfully joyful, then, will be that cry, when we hear that all our toils and cares are past—that sin shall no longer reign in the world! *Second*, the fate of our ungodly friends will be dreadful. All of us have ungodly friends, for whose conversion we pray. When that cry comes, it will be the knell of their souls; and yet for all that it will be a joyful day. In Matthew 24:32, it is compared to summer.

It will be the summer of the soul—the winter will be past. "Unto you that fear my name shall the Sun of righteousness arise with healing in his wings" (Mal. 4:2). "He shall be as the light of the morning, when the sun riseth, even a morning without clouds" (2 Sam. 23:4). "He shall come down like rain upon the mown grass: as showers that water the earth" (Ps. 72:6). But most of all, the cry, "The Bridegroom cometh," will revive the drooping hearts of His own chosen ones. It will remind us of the time that He chose us to be His own—the time of love when He wooed us and said: "Thou shalt be for me, and not for another man." He that loved us and died for us and promised to return and receive us to Himself—"Behold, the Bridegroom cometh." Ah! consider, beloved friends, whether it will be a time of joy to you or of wailing. Careless sinner, what shall then become of thee?

The Discovery

"Our lamps are gone out." A dry wick has often a great blaze for awhile. So hypocrites often keep up their profession to the last; often it is very showy and evident. Many things might awaken hypocrites.

1. Their case is described in sermons. Often the minister is directed by God to speak exactly to their case. Often the word comes very close to their conscience. We say, Surely that man will take the word home. No; it slips past some way or other.

2. Seeing others converted. Often hypocrites see others beside them undergo a saving change. They see them convinced of sin—made to lie in the dust—brought to Jesus—filled with joy—living a new life—overcoming the world. This might open their eyes to see that their professed change is false and hollow.

3. The death of others. It must be a solemn thing to a hypocrite to see others cut down. Death tears away every mask—it calls the soul before the heart-searching One. Pretended convictions, pretended grace, words of put-on godliness will not avail now. When hypocrites see others cut down, I have often thought, surely they

will turn now. Yet it is not so; they often burn on to the last. (a) They have gotten a name to live, and they do not like to lose it. They have made a profession, and they do not like to draw back from it. Ministers have been pleased and satisfied, or godly persons have esteemed them, and they do not like all at once to give up this. So Judas was long esteemed a true disciple and kept up his profession to the last. (b) Often do they delude themselves. They have some inward light and knowledge which they mistake for grace. They have a form of godliness—pray in secret and in the family and so deceive themselves as well as others. But their lamps will go out at the coming of Christ. "Our lamps are gone out"—not one blaze more—not one spark more. What is the reason?

1. *There is no indwelling grace.* Their lamps went out because they had no oil. They burned for a while, as a dry wick will do, often with a great blaze. But soon the flame decays and it goes out for want of oil. This is the case with hypocrites. They have no spring of gracious oil within their hearts. The Spirit of God often comes upon them, but He does not dwell in them. So it was with Balaam. His eyes were opened—he saw much of the joy of God's people—he longed to die the death of the righteous (Num. 24:22); but he had no oil in the lamp, and his lamp went out. So with Saul. "God gave him another heart" and "the Spirit of God came upon him" (1 Sam. 10:9–10); but he had no oil in the lamp—no gracious indwelling of the Spirit enabling him to cleave to Jesus, and so his lamp went out. Often, in a rainy season, there are large pools of water gathered in the field where there is no spring or fountain. At first they appear large and deep, but when the summer comes, they dry up and disappear. So it is with hypocrites in this congregation. Many of you have had the Spirit poured on you as it was on Balaam and on Saul—your eyes have been opened—you have had deep convictions, wonderful discoveries, panting desires after Christ and divine things. Yet you have never been brought by the working of the Spirit of God to cleave to

Christ. Ah! your lamp will go out and leave you in the blackness of darkness.

Dear friends! make sure of a deep and real work of grace upon your hearts. Remember, it is said that the man who built his house upon the rock digged deep and laid his foundation on the rock. It is not every change that is saving conversion. Of many it is true, "They return, but not to the most High" (Hos. 7:16). Do not be contented with being civilized if you are not converted. It will not stand you in stead in the great day.

2. *They have to appear before Christ.* It is an easy thing to appear a Christian before men: "Man looks only on the outward appearance, but God looketh on the heart." As long as hypocrites have to appear only before men, they can keep up appearances. They can talk and read and pray as if they were God's children; but when the cry comes, "Behold, the Bridegroom cometh," then they know that they must appear before Christ, the searcher of hearts. When Jesse brought in his seven sons before Samuel, he looked on Eliab and said: "Surely the Lord's anointed is before me." But God said: "I have refused him: for the LORD seeth not as man seeth; for man looketh on the outward appearance, but the LORD looketh on the heart" (1 Sam. 16:7).

Ah, friends! There are many of you that can now come in boldly before men, though you know yourselves to be graceless—never born again—living in sin. You can sit down at a sacrament without fear or shame; but when Christ comes, your lamp will go out—you will not be able to bear the glance of His holy eye. O pray for such an interest in Christ now, that you may stand before the Son of Man at His coming!

The Anxious Application

"Give us of your oil; for our lamps are gone out."

1. *Hypocrites will then see the difference between them and the godly.* Their lamps will be out, but the lamps of the truly godly will be burning bright and clear. At present, hypocrites think they are as good as anyone. They think there is no real difference between them

and God's people. In that day they will be convinced that there is a great gulf fixed between.

2. *They will see what a happy thing it is to have oil in their lamp.* At present, many among you do not see your need of grace. You do not see that you would be any happier with grace in your heart. You are willing rather to remain as you are. But in that day you will cry: "Give us of your oil." You will see the peace of the godly in that day. They will be unmoved amid a falling universe. The blood of Christ on their conscience will give them abiding peace. You will see their joyful faces as they hear the cry, as they hear the footsteps, of the coming Bridegroom—you will hear their song of praise as they welcome their Lord and Redeemer. At present the godly are poor and despised, often in trouble and chastened every morning, and you would not join them. But in that day they will be like the stones of a crown— like the children of a king.

3. *They will apply to the godly.* At present, hypocrites despise the godly and would not apply to them for anything. When a truly godly person warns you or advises you, you are offended. But in that day you will be in despair—glad to apply to anyone. You will be glad to apply to godly friends and godly ministers in that day. You that wonder what makes people go to speak to ministers, you that mock and deride the truly godly, you will say: "Give us of your oil." At this day ministers and godly friends knock at your door, beseeching you to get the oil of grace into your hearts. But at that day you will knock at their door, crying, "Give us of your oil; for our lamps are gone out."

O what folly to rest in desires after grace, when even hypocrites will have this in that awful day!

The Disappointment

"Not so, lest there be not enough for us and you."

1. *It is not in their power to give grace.* It pleases God to use the godly as instruments, but He has not given them to be fountains of grace: "I have planted, Apollos watered; but God gave the increase. So then

neither is he that planteth anything, neither he that watereth; but God that giveth the increase" (1 Cor. 3:6–7). Rachel said to Jacob: "Give me children, or else I die. And Jacob's anger was kindled against Rachel: and he said, Am I in God's stead?" (Gen. 30:1–2). So grace is not in the hand of man. Those who receive Christ "[are] born, not of blood, nor of the will of the flesh, nor of the will of man, but of God" (John 1:13). It is in vain, then, that you look to the means to give saving grace to your soul. The ax cannot hew without the hand of the forester. The pitcher that carries water is not the well. It will be in vain that you apply to God's children in that awful day. Go to Jesus now.

2. *They have none to spare.* The righteous scarcely are saved. Every child of God gets just so much grace as will carry him to heaven and no more. Even now every child of God feels that he has nothing to spare. He has not too much of the Holy Spirit helping him to pray—to mourn over sin—to love Christ. In time of temptation a believer feels as if he had nothing of the Holy Spirit. He has more need to receive than ability to give away. When Christ shall come in that solemn hour, He will feel that He has none to spare.

Oh, dear friends! Go and buy for yourselves. You that know yourselves graceless, go, before the cry is made, to Jesus and get grace for yourselves. The saints cannot give it you—ministers cannot give it you. All our springs are in Jesus. In Him the Spirit dwells without measure. Lord, incline their hearts to run to You!

Who Is Ready?

All are not ready. This parable shows that all who make a profession of being Christ's are not ready. The foolish virgins appeared to be ready. They had their robe, their lamp, their wick, and flame, yet they were not ready. It is not all of you that seem to be Christians that are ready. Many of you come to the house of God and sit down at sacraments and make a profession of care for your soul; yet you are not ready. Not all who are anxious are ready. The foolish were anxious now.

They had a throbbing heart—they went to buy—their cry was loud and bitter—perhaps they shed bitter tears; yet they were not ready. Many of you are anxious—going to buy. You have wet cheeks when you go to seek the Lord; yet you are not ready. If you were to die tonight, or if Christ were to come tonight, you would not be found ready. Who, then, is ready?

1. *Those who have the wedding garment.* This you see in Revelation 19:7–8: "His wife hath made herself ready. And to her was granted that she should be arrayed in fine linen, clean and white: for the fine linen is the righteousness of the saints." And Psalm 45:9, 13: "Upon thy right hand did stand the queen in gold of Ophir. . . . The king's daughter is all glorious within: her clothing is of wrought gold." And in Matthew 22:11, we find this was the first thing that struck the eye of the king, that the man had not on a wedding garment. This wedding garment is the righteousness of God—the skirt of Jesus cast over the soul—the imputed righteousness. This is the first part of readiness to meet the heavenly Bridegroom. Have you been shown your own utter loathsomeness? That you are all as an unclean thing, all vile and filthy? Have you gotten a glorious discovery of the way of righteousness by what Christ has done being reckoned to us? Have you lain down under the blood and white robe of the Lord Jesus? Then you are ready.

Do not mistake. (a) It is not the knowledge of this imputed righteousness. Many people hear and know a great deal about this robe of righteousness who never put it on and are not a whit the better. Knowledge will but condemn you and sink you deeper. (b) It is not a desire to have this righteousness. The sluggard desires and has nothing. Many have lazy desires after Christ that are never satisfied, and they are none the better for them—like beggars wishing they were rich. (c) It is not having it once put over us and then something else afterward. (d) This fine linen must be granted to us forever. It is not that Christ is our righteousness at first, and our own holiness after; but it is Christ to the end. Our wedding garment in heaven must be Christ's blood-washed robe; we must have it granted to us every day—every moment. Happy soul, who daily beholds your own vileness and daily receives that wedding garment to hide your nakedness.

2. *Those who have the new heart.* Can two walk together except they be agreed? It is impossible that two souls can be happy together if they love opposite things. It is like two bullocks in the yoke drawing different ways. Hence the deep wisdom of the command which forbids God's children to intermarry with the world. What fellowship has light with darkness? In the same way with Christ's bride. She must be of one mind with Him if she would enter in with Him to the marriage.

Suppose one of you who has an old heart were to be admitted with Christ to the marriage. Your heart is enmity to God—you hate God's people—the Sabbath is a weariness—you serve divers lusts and pleasures— the Lamb that is in the midst of the throne would lend you, and God would wipe away tears from your eyes; but you hate God and the Lamb—how could you be happy there? None but God's children or companions (psalm-singing hypocrites, as you used to call them)— could you be happy with them? An eternal Sabbath!— my highest notion of heaven is an eternal Sabbath with Christ—could you be happy? Could you enjoy it? Ah, my friends! There shall in no wise enter in any that defile—any that make or love a lie. If you are still unsaved, you are not ready.

3. *Those whose lamps are trimmed.* While the wise virgins slept, they were not ready. True, they had the wedding garment and the oil in their vessels; but their lamps were dim—their eyes were closed. But when they heard the cry they arose and trimmed their lamps, and now they are ready to meet and enter with the Bridegroom. It is not every child of God that is ready. Is a backslider ready—one that has gathered fresh guilt upon the soul and has not gotten it washed away—one that is still lying under guilt and not hastening to the

Fountain—one that is standing with his back to the house of God and his face toward his idol? Is an idolater ready—one that once loved Christ and now puts an idol in his place—entangled with some unlawful affection? Is the soul ready that has left its first love—grown cold in divine things? Was Solomon ready when his heart went after many wives? Or Peter, when he denied his Lord?

Ah! Learn, dear friends, to stir up the grace that is in you. Stir up your faith in Jesus—your love to Him and to the saints, if you would be ready. Watch! Live among divine things—keep the eye open to the coming glory.

The Reward of Those Who Are Ready

"They went in with him to the marriage."

1. *Christ will own them.* Christ will take them in with Him before His Father and say: "Behold, I, and the children whom thou hast given me." These are they for whom I died, prayed, reigned. At present Christ does not publicly own His people, or put a difference between them and hypocrites. (a) The world does not know them. The sun shines on the evil and on the good. Worldly men think we are like themselves. (b) Saints do not know us. Often they suspect us. Often the children of God suspect one another unjustly. They have not this or that experience—this or that mark of God's children. (c) Often we know not ourselves. When the war of corruption is strong within—when we have fallen into sin—when grace is low in the soul—"Can I deem myself a child?" But then Christ will own us and that will put an end to all doubt forever and ever. The scoffing world will then know that Christ loved us—they will then wish they had cast in their lot with us. The saints will see that we are Christ's as well as they. They will have no more suspicions of us. We will have no more doubts of ourselves—no more deadness, inconsistency, corruption, darkness, sin. Christ will confess our name before His Father. He will say: "Come, ye blessed of my Father; inherit the kingdom prepared for you."

2. *Saints shall be with Christ*: "Went in with him."
The greatest joy of a believer in this world is to enjoy
the presence of Christ—not seen, not felt, not heard,
but still real—the real presence of the unseen Savior.
It is this that makes secret prayer sweet, and sermons sweet, and sacraments sweet, when we meet
with Jesus in them: "I have set the Lord always before me. Because he is at my right hand, I shall not
be moved." Often Jesus hides His face and we are
troubled. We seek Him whom our soul loves, but He
is gone. We rise and seek, but find Him not. At the
best, it is but half bliss to feel after an unseen Savior.
Suppose a husband and wife are parted by many seas.
It is sweet to have letters and love tokens, and to see
a friend who left him well; but this will not make up
for his presence. So we mourn an absent Lord. But
when He comes we shall be with Him. "In thy presence is fulness of joy; at thy right hand there are
pleasures forevermore" (Ps. 16:11). Here we have drops
and gleams of pleasure. Christ could not be happy
without us. We are His body. If one child of God were
wanting, He would not be complete. We are His fullness. Hence His prayer: "Father, I will that they also,
whom thou hast given me, be with me where I am;
that they may behold my glory, which thou hast given
me" (John 17:24). We could not be happy without
Christ. Take us to the golden pavement, the pearly
gates, the songs, the thrones, the palms, the angel—
we would still say, Where is the God-man that died
for me? Where is the Angel that redeemed me from
all evil? Where is Jesus? Where is the side that was
pierced? "We shall see his face." The Lamb is the light
thereof. We shall stand with the Lamb upon mount
Zion—we shall never be parted more.

The Fate of Hypocrites

"The door was shut." The door of Christ stands wide
open for a long time, but shuts at last. When Christ
comes, the door will be shut. Now the door is open and
we are sent to invite you to come in. Soon it will be

shut and then you cannot. So it was at the flood. One hundred and twenty years the door of the ark stood wide open. Noah went forth, and preached everywhere, inviting men to come in. The Spirit strove with men. But they only mocked at the coming flood. At last the day came. Noah entered, and God shut him in. The door was shut. The flood came and carried them all away. So it will be with many here. The door is wide open now. Jesus says: "I am the door: by me if any man enter in, he shall be saved, and shall go in and out, and find pasture." Christ does not say, I was, or I will be, but, I am the door. At present any man may enter in. Soon Christ will come—like a thief—like a snare—like travail on a woman with child—and you shall not escape. Enter in at the strait gate.

They prayed, "Lord, Lord, open to us." At present, hypocrites do not pray, or not in earnest. They have a cold, formal, dull prayer; but in that day they shall cry in real earnest. At present, many of you would be ashamed to be seen in earnest about your soul—weeping or praying or going to a minister. In that day you will lose all shame—you will weep and howl and run to Christ's door in agony of spirit. At present many of you are sought after by Christ: "He is come to seek and to save that which was lost." He is the shepherd seeking the one sheep that was lost. He stands at your door and knocks—stands and cries: "Unto you, O men, I call"— "Turn ye, turn ye"—Sinner, sinner, open to me. In that day it will be the very reverse. You will seek after the Savior in that day and not find Him—you will stand and knock at His door—you will exert your voice and cry: "Lord, Lord, open to me." What a scene this parish will present in that day! Those who come not to the house of God—old men and old women, gray headed in carelessness and sin—young persons, mad upon pleasure—children, who live without Christ—you will be all in earnest on that day. May this not rebuke some of you that pray not, or pray in a cold, dull manner, or in a form? Ah! You will pray in that day, when too late. Why not antedate that anxiety and begin to pray now?

They were disappointed. The Lord answered: "I know you not." Christ will own His own people: "I know them." The poor despised believers He will own. Though the world knew them not, Christ will know them. Not one shall be passed over in that day. But not so with the foolish virgins who have no oil in their lamps. Christ will not own them. Ah! It will be a fearful thing to be denied by Christ before His Father and the holy angels. "Watch, therefore; for ye know neither the day nor the hour when the Son of Man cometh." See that ye have true grace in your hearts—that Christ is your righteousness—that your soul is alive.

The Two Debtors

Alexander Maclaren (1826–1910) was one of Great Britain's most famous preachers. While pastoring the Union Chapel, Manchester (1858–1903), he became known as "the prince of expository preachers." Rarely active in denominational or civic affairs, Maclaren invested his time in studying the Word in the original languages and sharing its truths with others in sermons that are still models of effective expository preaching. He published a number of books of sermons and climaxed his ministry by publishing his monumental *Expositions of Holy Scripture*.

This message is taken from *Maclaren's Expositions of Holy Scripture*.

Alexander Maclaren

9

THE TWO DEBTORS

Luke 7:41–43

WE ALL KNOW the lovely story in which this parable is embedded. A woman of notoriously bad character had somehow come in contact with Jesus Christ, and had by Him been aroused from her sensuality and degradation, and calmed by the assurance of forgiveness. So, when she heard that He was in her own town, what could she do but hasten to the Pharisee's house and brave the cruel, scornful eyes of the eminently respectable people that would meet her there? She carries with her part of the spoils and instruments of her sinful adornment to devote it to His service. But before she can open the cruse, her heart opens, and the hot tears flow on His feet, inflicting an indignity where she had meant an honor. She has nothing at hand to repair the fault. She will not venture to take her poor garment, which might have done it; but with a touch she loosens her long hair, and with the ingenuity and self-abasement of love, uses that for a towel. Then, gathering confidence from her reception and carried further than she had meant, she ventures to lay her sinful lips on His feet, as if asking pardon for the tears that would come—the only lips, except those of the traitor, that are recorded as having touched the Master. And only then does she dare to pour upon Him her only wealth.

What says the Pharisee? Has he a heart at all? He is scandalized at such a scene at his respectable table. And no wonder, for he could not have known that a change had passed upon the woman, and her evil repute was obviously notorious. He does not wonder at her having found her way into his house, for the meal was half public. But he began to doubt whether a Man who tolerates such familiarities from such a person could be a prophet or, if He were, whether He could be a good man. "He would have known her if He had been a prophet," thinks he. The thought is only a questionably true one. "If He had known her, He would have thrust her back with His foot," he thinks; that thought is obviously false. But Simon's righteousness was of the sort that gathers up its own robes about it, and shoves back the poor sinner into the filth. "She is a sinner," says he. No, Simon! She *was* a sinner, but she *is* a penitent and is on the road to be a saint. Having been washed, she is a great deal cleaner than you who are only white-washed.

Our Lord's parable is the answer to the Pharisee's thought, and in it Jesus shows Simon that He knows him and the woman a great deal better than he did. There are three things to which briefly I ask your attention: the common debt, in varying amounts; the common insolvency; and the love, like the debt, varying in amount. Now, note these things in order.

The Common Debt

I do not propose to dwell at all upon that familiar metaphor, familiar to us all from its use in the Lord's Prayer, by which sin and the guilt of sin are shadowed forth for us in an imperfect fashion by the conception of debt. For duty neglected is a debt to God, which can only be discharged by a penalty. And all sin, and its consequent guilt and exposure to punishment, may be regarded under the image of indebtedness.

But the point that I want you to notice is that these two in our parable, though they are meant to be portraits of Simon and the woman, are also representatives of the two classes to one or other of which we all belong. They are both debtors, though one owes but a tenth of what the other does. That is to say, our Lord here draws a broad distinction between people who are outwardly respectable, decent, cleanly living, and people who have fallen into the habit and are living a life of gross and open transgression. There has been a great deal of very pernicious loose representation of the attitude of Christianity in reference to this matter, common in evangelical pulpits. And I want you to observe that our Lord draws a broad line and says, "Yes! you, Simon, are a great deal better than that woman was. She was coarse, unclean, her innocence gone, her purity stained. She had been wallowing in filth, and you, with your respectability, your rigid morality, your punctilious observance of the ordinary human duties, you were far better than she was and had far less to answer for than she had." Fifty is only a tenth of five hundred. There is a broad distinction, which nothing ought to be allowed to obliterate, between people who, without religion, are trying to do right, to keep themselves in the paths of morality and righteousness, to discharge their duty to their fellows, controlling their passions and their flesh; and others who put the reins upon the necks of the horses and let them carry them where they will, and live in an eminent manner for the world and the flesh and the Devil. And there is nothing in evangelical Christianity which in the smallest degree obliterates that distinction, but rather it emphasizes it and gives a man full credit for any difference that there is in his life and conduct and character between himself and the man of gross transgression.

But then it says, on the other side, the difference which does exist, and is not to be minimized, is, after all, a difference of degree. They are both debtors. They stand in the same relation to the creditor, though the amount of the indebtedness is extremely different. We are all sinful men, and we stand in the same relation to God, though one of us may be much darker and blacker than the other.

And then, remember, that when you begin to talk about the guilt of actions in God's sight, you have to go far below the mere surface. If we could see the infinite complexity of motives—aggravations on the one side and palliations on the other—which go to the doing of a single deed, we should not be so quick to pronounce that the publican and the harlot are worse than the Pharisee. It is quite possible that an action which passes muster in regard to the morality of the world may, if regard be had (which God only can exercise) to the motive for which it is done, be as bad as, if not worse than, the lust and the animalism, drunkenness and debauchery, crime and murder, which the vulgar scales of the world consider to be the heavier. If you once begin to try to measure guilt, you will have to pass under the surface appearance, and will find that many a white and dazzling act has a very rotten inside, and that many a very corrupt and foul one does not come from so corrupt a source as at first sight might seem to be its origin. Let us be very modest in our estimate of the varying guilt of actions. Remember that deep down below all diversities there lies a fundamental identity in which there is no difference. Remember that all of us respectable people that never broke a law of the nation, and scarcely ever a law of propriety, in our lives, and the outcasts, if there are any here now—the drunkards, the sensualists—all of us stand in this respect in the same class. We are all debtors, for we have "all sinned and come short of the glory of God." A viper an inch long and the thickness of whipcord has a sting and poison in it, and is a viper. And if the question is whether a man has smallpox or not, one pustule is as good evidence as if he was spotted all over. So, remember, he who owes five hundred and he who owes the tenth part of it, which is fifty, are both debtors.

The Common Insolvency

"They had nothing to pay." Well, if there is no money—"no effects" in the bank, no cash in the till, nothing to distrain upon—it does not matter very much what the amount of the debt is, seeing that there is nothing to meet it. Whether it is fifty or five hundred the man is equally unable to pay. And that is precisely our position.

I admit, of course, that men without any recognition of God's pardoning mercy, or any of the joyful impulse that comes from the sense of Christ's redemption, or any of the help that is given by the indwelling of the Spirit who sanctifies may do a great deal in the way of mending their characters and making themselves purer and nobler. But that is not the point which my text contemplates, because it deals with a past. And the fact that lies under the metaphor of my text is this, that none of us can in any degree diminish our sin considered as a debt to God. What can you and I do to lighten our souls of the burden of guilt? What we have written we have written. Tears will not wash it out and amendment will not alter the past that stands frowning and irrevocable. If there be a God at all, then our consciences, which speak to us of demerit, proclaim guilt in its two elements—the sense of having done wrong and the foreboding of punishment therefore. Guilt cannot be dealt with by the guilty one; it must be Someone else who deals with it. He, and only He against whom we have sinned, can touch the great burden that we have piled upon us.

We have nothing to pay. We may mend our ways, but that does not touch the past. We may hate the evil, that will help to keep us from doing it in the future, but it does not affect our responsibility for what is done. We cannot touch it. There it stands irrevocable with this solemn sentence written over the black pile, "Every transgression and disobedience shall receive its just recompense of reward." We have nothing to pay.

But my text suggests, further, that a condition precedent to forgiveness is the recognition by us of our penniless insolvency. Though it is not distinctly stated, it is clearly and necessarily implied in the narrative, that the two debtors are to be supposed as having come and held out a couple of pairs of empty hands and sued *in formâ pauperis*. You must recognize your insolvency if you expect to be forgiven. God does not accept dividends, so much in the pound, and let you off the rest on consideration thereof. If you are going to pay, you have to pay all; if He is going to forgive, you have to let Him forgive all. It must be one thing or the other. You and I have to elect which of the two we shall stand by and which of the two shall be applied to us.

Oh, dear friends! may we all come and say,

> Nothing in my hand I bring,
> Simply to Thy Cross I cling.

The Love Which Varies with the Forgiveness

"Tell Me which of them will love him most." Simon does not penetrate Christ's design. There is a dash of supercilious contempt for the story and the question, as it seems to me, in the languid, half-courteous answer: "I suppose, if it were worth my while to think about such a thing, that he to whom he forgave the most." He did not know what a battery was going to be unmasked. Jesus says, "Thou hast rightly judged."

The man that is most forgiven is the man that will love most. Well, that answer is true if all other things about the two debtors are equal. If they are the same sort of men, with the same openness to sentiments of gratitude and generosity, the man who is let off the smaller debt will generally be less obliged than the man who is let off the larger. But it is, alas, not always the case that we can measure benefits conferred by gratitude shown. Another element comes in—namely, the consciousness of the benefit received—which measures the gratitude far more accurately than the actual benefit bestowed. And so we must take both these things, the actual amount of forgiveness, so to speak, which is conferred, and the depth of the sense of the forgiveness received, in order to get the measure of the love which answers it. This principle breaks up into two thoughts, of which I have only just a word or two to say.

First, it is very often true that the greatest sinners make the greatest saints. There have been plenty of instances all down the history of the world—and there are plenty of instances, thank God, cropping up every day still—in which some poor, wretched outcast, away out in the darkness, living on the husks that the swine do eat and liking to be in the pigsty, is brought back into the Father's house, and turns out a far more loving son and a far better servant than the man that had never wandered away from it. "The publicans and the harlots" do often yet "go into the kingdom of God before" the respectable people.

So let no outcast man or woman listening to me now despair. You can come back from the furthest darkness. Whatever ugly things you have in your memories and your consciences, you may make them stepping-stones on which to climb to the very throne of God. Let no respectable people despise the outcasts. There may be the making in them of far better Christians than we are.

But, on the other hand, let no man think lightly of sin. Though it can be forgiven and swept away, and the gross sinner may become the great saint, there will be scars and bitter memories and habits surging up again after we thought they were dead. The old ague and fever that we caught in the pestilential land will hang by us when we have migrated into a more wholesome climate. It is never good for a man to have sinned, even though, through his sin, God may have taken occasion to bring him near to Himself.

But the second form of this principle is always true— namely, that those who are most conscious of forgiveness will be most fruitful of love. The depth and fervor of our individual Christianity depends more largely on the clearness of our consciousness of our own personal guilt and the firmness of our grasp of forgiveness than upon anything else.

Why is it that such multitudes of you professing Christians are such icebergs in your Christianity? Mainly for this reason—that you have never found out, in anything like an adequate measure, how great a sinner you are, and how sure and sweet and sufficient Christ's pardoning mercy is. And so you are like Simon—you will ask Jesus to dinner, but you will not give Him any water for His feet or ointment for His head. You will do the conventional and necessary pieces of politeness, but not one act of impulse from the heart ever comes from you. You discharge "the duties of religion." What a phrase! You discharge the duties of religion. Ah! if you had been down into the horrible pit and the miry clay, and had seen a hand and a face looking down, and an arm outstretched to lift you; if you had ever known what the rapture was after that subterraneous experience of having your feet set upon a rock and your goings established, you would come to Him and you would say, "Take me all, O Lord! For I am all redeemed by Thee." "To whom little is forgiven the same loveth little." Does not that explain the imperfect Christianity of thousands of us?

Fifty pence and five hundred pence are both small sums. Our Lord had nothing to do here with the absolute amount of debt, but only with the comparative amount of the two debts. But when He wanted to tell the people what the absolute amount of the debt was, He did it in that other story of the Unfaithful Servant. He owed his lord, not fifty pence (fifty-eight pences or thereabouts), not five hundred pence, but "ten thousand talents," which comes to near two and a half million of English money. And that is the picture of our indebtedness to God. "We have nothing to pay." Here is the payment—that Cross, that dying Christ. Turn your faith there, and then you will get ample forgiveness that will kindle love and that will overflow in service. For the aperture in the heart at which forgiveness enters in is precisely of the same width as the one at which love goes out. Christ has loved us all and perfectly. Let us love Him back again who has died that we might live and borne our sins in His own body.

NOTES

The Parable of the Prodigal Son

David Martyn Lloyd-Jones (1898–1981) was born in
Wales and was taken to London in 1914. There he
trained for a medical career and was associated with
the famous Dr. Thomas Horder in Harley Street. He
abandoned medicine for the Gospel ministry, and from
1927 to 1938 he served the Presbyterian Church at
Sanfields, Aberavon, Wales. In 1938, he became
associate minister with Dr. G. Campbell Morgan at the
Westminster Chapel, London; and in 1943, when
Morgan retired, Lloyd-Jones succeeded him. His
expositions of the Scriptures attracted great crowds
wherever he preached. He retired in 1968 to devote his
time to writing and limited itinerant ministry.
Calvinistic in doctrine, he emphasized the "plight of
man and the power of God to save."

This message is taken from *Evangelistic Sermons*,
published in 1983 by Banner of Truth Trust, Edinburgh.

David Martyn Lloyd-Jones

10

THE PARABLE OF THE PRODIGAL SON

Luke 15:11–32

THERE IS NO parable or saying of our Lord which is quite as well-known and as familiar as the parable of the prodigal son. No parable is quite so frequently quoted in religious discussions, or made use of in order to support various theories and contentions with respect to these matters. All schools of thought seem to claim a right to it; it is held to prove all sorts of theories and ideas which are mutually destructive and which exclude one another. It is quite clear, therefore, that the parable can be very easily and readily mishandled and misinterpreted. How can we avoid that danger? What are the principles that should guide us as we come to interpret it? It seems to me that there are two fundamental principles which must be observed and which, if observed, will guarantee a correct interpretation.

The first is that we must always beware of interpreting any portion of Scripture in such a manner as to come into conflict with the general teaching of Scripture elsewhere. The New Testament must be approached as a whole. It is a complete and entire revelation given by God through His servants; a revelation which has been revealed in parts and sections, all of which go together to make a complete whole. There are obviously, therefore, no contradictions between these various parts, no clashes, no irreconcilable passages and statements. This is not to say that we can understand every single statement. What I do say is that there are no contradictions in Scripture. To suggest that the teachings of Jesus Christ and Paul, or the teachings of Paul and the other apostles, do not agree is subversive of the entire claim of the New Testament itself and of the claim of the church for it throughout the centuries, until the rise of the so-called higher-critical school some hundred years ago. I need not go into this matter this evening. Let it suffice to say that it is only the more superficial critics, who are by now many years behind the times, who still try to make and force an antithesis between what they call "the religion of Jesus" and the "faith of St. Paul." Scripture is to be compared with Scripture. Every theory we evolve must be tested by the solid body of doctrine and dogma which is to be found in the entire Bible and which has been defined by the church. Were this simple rule remembered, the vast majority of the heresies would never have arisen.

The second rule is a little more particular. It is that we should always avoid the danger of drawing any negative conclusions from the teaching of a parable. This applies not only to this particular parable, but to all parables. A parable is never meant to be a full outline of truth. Its business is to convey one great lesson, to present one big aspect of positive truth. That being its object and purpose, nothing is so foolish as to draw negative conclusions from it. That certain things are not said in the parable means nothing. A parable is important, and matters only, not from the point of view of what it does not say, but from the point of view of what it does say. Its value is entirely and exclusively positive and in no respect negative. Now I suggest to you that the failure to remember that simple rule has been responsible for most of the strange and fantastic theories and ideas which have been propounded supposedly on the basis of the parable of the prodigal son. That this should have been possible at all is surely astonishing, for if those who have done this had only looked at the two other parables which are in the same chapter, they would have seen at once how unjustifiable was their procedure. Why not draw negative conclusions from those · also? And so with all parables?

But apart from that, how utterly ridiculous and illogical it is to base and found your system of doctrine upon what is not said. How dishonest it is! For it does away with all authority and leaves you with no standard save your own prejudice and your own desire and your own imagination. Now that, I say, is what has been done so frequently with this parable. Let me illustrate that by reminding you of some of the false conclusions that have been drawn from it. Is this not the parable to which they constantly refer who try to prove that ideas of justice and judgment and wrath are utterly and entirely foreign to God's nature and to Jesus' teaching concerning Him? "There is nothing here," they say, "of the father's wrath, nor the father's demands for certain actions on the part of the son—just love, pure love, nothing but love." This is a typical example of a negative conclusion drawn from the parable. Because it does not positively teach the justice and the wrath of God, we are told that such qualities do not belong to God at all. That Jesus Christ elsewhere emphasizes these qualities is of course also completely and entirely ignored.

Another example is the way in which we are told that this parable does away with the absolute necessity for repentance. I have heard of a preacher who tried to prove that the prodigal was a humbug even when he returned home. He stated that the prodigal had decided to say something which sounded right, though he did not believe it at all, in order to impress his father—that his exact repetition of the words proves the case. The ultimate point is that in spite of this, in spite of a sham repetition, in spite of all, the father forgave. The final clinching argument of this preacher was that the father said nothing about repentance. Therefore, because he said nothing, it does not matter; because repentance is not taught and impressed upon the son by the father, repentance toward God does not matter!

But perhaps the most serious of all the false conclusions is that which tells us that no mediator between God and man is necessary, and that the idea of atonement is foreign to the Gospel and is to be attributed rather to the legalistic mind of Paul. "There is no mention in the parable," they say, "of anyone coming between the father and the son. There is no talk at all about another paying a ransom, or making an atonement; just the direct dealing between father and son conditioned solely upon the latter's return from the far country." Because those things are not specifically mentioned and stressed in the parable, it is agreed that they do not count at all and really do not matter. As if our Lord's object in the parable was to give a complete outline of the whole of the Christian truth and not just to teach one aspect of the truth. Surely it must be obvious to you that if a like procedure were adopted in the case of all parables, the position would be utterly chaotic and we should be faced with a mass of contradictions.

The business of a parable then is to present to us and to teach us one great positive truth. And if ever that should be clear and self-evident, it is in this particular case. It is no mere accident that this parable is one of three parables. Our Lord seems to have gone out of His way to protect us against the very danger to which I have been referring. But apart even from that, the key to the whole situation is provided in the first two verses of the chapter which provide us with the essential background and context. "Then drew near unto him all the publicans and sinners for to hear him. And the Pharisees and scribes murmured, saying, This man receiveth sinners, and eateth with them." Then follow these three parables, obviously dealing with that precise situation and obviously meant to reply to the murmurings of the Pharisees and scribes. And, as if to enforce it still further, our Lord draws a certain moral or conclusion at the end of each parable. The great point, surely, is that there is hope for all, that God's love extends even to the publicans and sinners. The glorious truth that shines out in these parables, and which is meant to be impressed upon us, is that amazing love of God, its scope and its reach, and especially by way of contrast to the ideas of the Pharisees and scribes on that subject.

The first two parables are designed to impress upon us the love of God as an activity which seeks out the sinner, that takes infinite trouble in order to find him and rescue him, and to show the joy of God and all the host of heaven when even one soul is saved. And then comes this parable of the prodigal son. Why this addition? Why the greater elaboration? Why a man, rather than a sheep or a lost coin? Surely there can be but one answer. As the first two parables have stressed God's activity alone without telling us anything about the actions or reactions or condition of the sinner, so this parable is spoken to impress that aspect and that side of the matter, lest anyone should be so foolish as to think that we should all be automatically saved by God's love even as the sheep and the lost coin were found. The great outstanding point is still the same, but its application is made more direct and more personal. What, then, is the teaching of this parable? What is its message to us this evening? Let us look at it along the following lines.

The Possibility of a New Beginning

The first truth it proclaims is *the possibility of a new beginning*, the possibility of a new start, a new opportunity, another chance. The very context and setting of the parable, as I have reminded you already, shows this perfectly. It was because they had sensed and seen this in His teaching that the publicans and sinners drew "nigh unto Him for to hear Him." They felt that there was a chance even for them, that in this man's teaching there was a new and a fresh hope. And even the Pharisees and scribes saw precisely the same thing. What annoyed them was that our Lord should have had anything at all to do with publicans and sinners. They had regarded such people as being utterly and entirely beyond hope and beyond redemption. That was the orthodox view to take of such people. They were so hopeless that they were to be entirely ignored. Religion was for good people and had nothing at all to do with bad people. It certainly had nothing to give them, and most certainly did not command good people to mix with bad people and treat them kindly and tell them of new possibilities. So the Pharisees and scribes were annoyed by our Lord's teaching. Anyone who saw any hope for a publican or sinner must, to them, be entirely wrong and a blasphemer. The same point exactly emerges in the parable in the different attitudes of the father and the elder brother toward the prodigal. The point being not as to how he should be received back, but rather as to whether he should be received back at all, whether he deserved anything at all.

That then is the thing which stands out on the very surface. There is a possibility of a new start, a new beginning, for all, even for the most desperate. No case can be worse than that of the prodigal son. Yet even he can start again. He has touched bottom, he has sunk to the very dregs, he has gone down so low that he could not possibly descend any further. Never has a more hopeless picture been drawn than that of this boy in the far country amidst the husks and the swine, penniless and friendless, utterly hopeless and forlorn, utterly desolate and dejected. But even he gets a fresh start, even he is called to make a new beginning. There is a turning-point which leads on to fortune and to happiness even for him. What a blessed Gospel, and especially in a world like this! What a difference the coming of Jesus Christ has made! What new hope for mankind appeared in Him! There is nothing that so demonstrates and proves that the Gospel of Jesus Christ is the only really optimistic philosophy and view of life offered to man, so much as the fact that publicans and sinners drew near to Him for to hear Him. And the message which they heard, as in this parable of the prodigal son, was something entirely new.

But I would have you note that it was not only new to the Jews and their leaders, but also new to the whole world. The hope held out to the vile and hopeless by the Gospel not only cut across the miserable system of the Jews, but also the philosophy of the Greeks. Those mighty men had been evolving their theories and their philosophies. Yet not one of them had anything to offer to the down and out. They all demanded a certain amount of intelligence and moral integrity and purity. They all had to postulate much in the human nature for which they catered. Nor were they realists. They wrote and spoke in a learned and fascinating manner about their utopias and their ideal states, but they left mankind exactly where it was, and were entirely divorced from ordinary life and living. The only people who have ever been in a position even to try the idealistic and humanistic methods of solving the problems of life have been the wealthy and the leisured, and even they have invariably found that they do not work. There was not, and there never had been, any hope for the hopeless in the world before Jesus Christ came. He alone taught the possibility of a new start and a new beginning.

But that teaching was not only new then during His days on earth, it is still new. And it is still surprising and astonishing and amazes the modern world quite as much as it amazed the ancient world of nearly two thousand years ago. For the world is still without hope and its controlling philosophy is still profoundly pessimistic. This is to be seen most clearly, perhaps, when it tries to be optimistic, for we see always that when it tries to comfort us it always has to point us to the future with its unknown possibilities. It tells us that in the new year things surely must be better, that they cannot at any rate be any worse. It argues that the depression must have lasted so long that surely the turn of the tide must of necessity be at hand. It is glad that one year has ended and that a new one is beginning.

What is the real secret of a new year? Its real secret lies in that we know nothing at all about it. All we know is bad, therefore we try to comfort ourselves by looking to what is unknown and by fondly imagining that it must be brighter and better. Then listen to it as it talks about its schemes and plans for the uplift of mankind. All it can tell you is that it is trying to make a better world for its children, trying to build for the future and for posterity. Always in the future! It can do nothing for itself, it can only hope to make things better for those who are yet unborn. And the longer it goes on talking about that and trying to do it, the more hesitant does it become. To prove this, just compare the language of 1875 with that of 1935, or even that of 1905 with 1935.

But if the situation is like that with regard to society in general, how infinitely more hopeless and filled with despair is it when we face it in a more individual and in a more personal sense! What has the world to offer by way of solution to the problems that tend to distress us most of all? The answer to that question is to be seen in the frantic efforts that men and women are making in their attempts to solve their problems. And yet nothing is more clearly seen than the fact that all their attempts are failures. Year after year men and women make their new resolutions. They realize that above all else what is needed is a fresh start and a new beginning. They decide to turn their backs on the past, to turn over a new leaf, or even to start a new book of life. That is their desire, that is their firm conviction and intention. They want to break with the past and for a time they do their utmost to do so, but it doesn't last. Gradually but inevitably they slide back to the old position and to the old state of affairs. After a few such experiences they no longer try, and come to the conclusion that all is hopeless. Up to a point, the fight is kept up and maintained, but sheer weariness and fatigue eventually overcome them. The pressure and the might of the world and its way seem to be entirely on the other side, and they give in. The position seems to be utterly hopeless.

I wonder how many there are, even in this service now, who feel like that in some respect or other! Do you feel that your life has gone wrong, has gone astray? Are you forever mocked by "the haunting specter of the might-have-been"? Do you feel that you have got yourself into such a position, and into such a situation, that you can never get out of it and put yourself right again? Do you feel that you are so far away from what you ought to be, and from what you would like to be, that you can never get there again? Do you feel hopeless about yourself because of some situation with which you are confronted, or because of some entanglement in which you have gotten involved, or because of some sin which has mastered you and which you cannot conquer? Have you turned to yourself and said, "What is the use of making any further effort, what is the use of trying again? I have tried and tried many and many a time before, but all to no purpose, and my trying now can lead to but the same result. I have made a mess of my life, I have forfeited my chance and my opportunity, and henceforth I have nothing to do but to make the best of a bad job." Are such your thoughts and your feelings? Is it your position that you have missed your opportunity in life, that what has been has been, that if only you had another chance things might be different, but that cannot be, and there it is? Is it that?

Alas! How many there are in such a position. How unhappy are the lives of the average man and woman. How hopeless! How sad! Now the very first word of the Gospel to all such is that they should lift up their heads, that all is not lost, that there is still hope. There is still the possibility of a new start and a new beginning here and now without any delay at all and without looking to the slightest extent on something imaginary which may belong to the unknown future. Lean upon something which happened nearly two thousand years ago but which is as strong and as powerful today as it was then. Even the prodigal can get right. There is a possible turning point even along the blackest and the most hopeless road. There is a new beginning offered even to publicans and sinners.

Definite Conditions Are Attached

But I must hasten to point out in detail what I have already indicated in passing, that this message of the Gospel is not something vague and general like the world's message, *but something to which definite conditions are attached.* And it is here we see most clearly why it was that our Lord spoke this particular parable in addition to the other two. To avail ourselves of this new beginning and new start which is offered by the Gospel, we must observe the following points. Let me impress upon you the importance of doing this. If you merely sit there and listen and allow yourselves to be moved in general by the glowing picture of the Gospel you will go home exactly as you were when you came. But if, on the other hand, you attend carefully and note each point and act upon it, you will find yourself going home an entirely different person. If you are anxious to avail yourself of the Gospel's new hope and new start, you must follow its methods and its instructions. What are they?

The first is that we must face our position squarely, honestly, and truly. It is one thing to be in a bad and difficult position, it is quite a different thing to face it honestly. This prodigal son had been in a thoroughly bad situation for a very long time before he truly realized it. A man does not suddenly get into that state in which he is described here. It happened gradually, almost unbeknown to himself. And even after it happened he did not properly realize it for some time. The process is so quiet and so insidious that the man himself scarcely sees it at all. He looks at his face in the mirror every day and does not see the changes that are taking place. It is someone who only sees him at intervals who sees the effects most clearly. And often when we begin to sense our terrible plight, we deliberately avoid thinking about it. We brush such thoughts aside and busy ourselves with other matters, more or less saying to ourselves as we do so, "What's the use of thinking, Here I am anyhow." Now the very first step back is to face the issue, to face the situation honestly and clearly. We are told that this young man "came to himself." That is actually what the man did! He faced things out with himself and did so quite frankly. He saw that his troubles were entirely due to his own actions and that he had been a fool. He saw that he should never have left his father, and should certainly never have treated him as he had done. He looked at himself and could scarcely believe that it really was himself. He looked at the husks and at the swine. He faced it right out.

Have you done that? Have you really looked at yourself? What if you put all your actions of the past year down on paper? What if you had kept a record of all your thoughts and desires, your ambitions and imaginings? Would you consent to their publication with your name beneath them? What are you now in comparison with what you once were? Look at your hands—are they clean? Look at your lips—are they pure? Look at your feet—where have they trodden, where have they been? Look at yourself! Is it really you? Then look around you at your position and surroundings! Do not shirk it! Be honest! What are you living on? Is it food or swine's husks? On what have you spent your money? For what purpose have you used money that should perhaps have gone to feed wife and children or to clothe them? On what have you been living? Look! Is it food fit for men? Look at what you enjoy. Face it calmly. Is it worthy of a creature created by God with intelligence and understanding? Does it honor man, leave alone God? Is it swine's food or is it really fit for human consumption? It is not enough that you should just bemoan your fate or feel miserable. How did you ever get into such a state and condition? Look at the swine and the husks and realize that it is all due to the fact that you have left your Father's house, that you have deliberately gone against your conscience, deliberately flouted religion and all its commands and dictates, that it has been entirely and utterly of your own doing. You are where you are today entirely as the result of your own choice and your own actions. Face that and admit it. That is the first essential step on the way back.

The next is to realize that there is only One to whom you can turn and only one thing to do. I need not work out that point in detail in connection with the prodigal. It is perfectly clear. "No man gave unto him." He had tried and had exhausted his own efforts and the efforts of all other people. He was finished and no one could help him. There was but one left. Father! The last, the only hope. The Gospel always insists upon our coming to that point. As long as you have a half-penny of your own left, the Gospel will not help you. As long as you have friends or agencies to which you can apply for help and which you believe can help you, the Gospel will give you nothing. Actually, of course, as long as a man thinks he can keep himself going by some of these other methods, he will continue to try to do so. And the world is still far from being bankrupt in our estimation. It still believes in its own methods and ideas. And how pathetically we cling to them! We bank on our own will-power and our own efforts. We draw upon the new years of our calendar as if they made the slightest difference to the actual state of affairs! We invoke the aid of friends and companions and of relations and dear ones. You know all about the process, not only in your attempts to put yourself right, but also in your attempts to put others right about whom you are concerned and worried. And on we will go until we have exhausted all. Like the prodigal we go on until we become frantic and until "no man gives unto us." Then and then only do we turn to God.

Oh, how foolish! Let me try to explode the fallacy here and now. Face it frankly. Realize that all your efforts must fail as they have always failed. Realize that the improvement will only be transient and temporary. Cease to fool yourself. Realize how desperate the position is. Realize further that there is only one power that can put you right—the power of Almighty God. You can go on trusting to yourself and others and trying with all your might. But a year from tonight the position will not only be the same, but actually worse. God alone can save you.

But as you turn to Him, you must realize further that you can plead nothing before Him save His mercy and His compassion. As the prodigal left home his great word was "give." He demanded his rights. He was full of self-confidence and even had a feeling that he was not being given his due and his rights. "Give!" But when he returns home, his vocabulary has changed and his word now is "make." Before, he felt he was someone and somebody and something that could demand rights worthy of itself and of himself. Now he feels he is nobody and nothing, and realizes that his first need is to be made into something. "Make me!" If you feel that you have any right to demand pardon and forgiveness from God, I can assure you that you are damned and lost. If you feel that it is God's business and God's duty to forgive you, you will most certainly not be forgiven. If you feel God is hard, and against you, you are guilty of the greatest sin of all. If you feel still that you are somebody and that you have a right to say "give," you will receive nothing but misery and continued wretchedness. But if you realize that you have sinned against God and angered Him; if you feel you are a worm and less, and unworthy even of the name of man, quite apart from being unworthy of God; if you feel you are nothing in view of the way you have left Him and turned your back upon Him, and ignored Him and flouted Him; if you just cast yourself upon Him and His mercy, asking Him if in His infinite goodness and kindness He can possibly make something of you, all will be different. God never desired to see you as you now are. It was against His wish and His will that you have wandered away. It is all of your own doing. Tell Him so and tell Him further that what worries and distresses you most of all is not merely the misery you have brought upon yourself, but the fact that you have disobeyed Him and insulted Him and wronged Him.

Then having realized all this, act upon it. Leave the far country. You have stood up in the field of the swine and the husks by your mere action in visiting this chapel. But walk right out of that far country. Leave the swine and the husks. Turn your back upon sin and give yourself to God. Feelings and desires and inclinations will avail you nothing. Do it! Make a break. Get to God and get right with God! Take your stand. Commit yourself! Venture on Him! Trust Him! How ridiculous it would have been for the prodigal to have thought of all he did and yet not do it! He would still have remained in the far country. But he did it. He acted upon his decision. He carried out his resolution. He went to his father and cast himself upon his mercy and compassion. You must do the same in the way I have already indicated.

A Real, Solid New Beginning and New Start

If you but do so, you will find that in your case, as in the case of the prodigal, *there will be a real, solid new beginning and new start.* The impossible will happen, and you will be amazed and astounded at what you will discover. I pass over the joy and the happiness and the thrill of it all tonight in order that I may impress upon you the reality of the new start which the Gospel gives. It is not something light and airy. It is no mere matter of sentiment or feelings. It is no mere drug or anesthetic which dulls our senses and therefore makes us dream of some bright realm. It is real and actual. In Jesus Christ a real genuine new start and new beginning are possible. And they are possible in Him alone! The greatness of the father's love in the parable is seen not so much in his attitude as in what he did. Love is no mere vague sentiment or general disposition. Love is active. It is the mightiest activity in the world and it transforms everything. That is why here also the love of God alone can really give us a new start and a new chance. The love of God does not merely talk about a new beginning, it makes a new beginning. "God so loved the world that He *gave*." The father did things to the prodigal; God alone can do that to us and for us which can set us on our feet again. Let us observe how He does it. Oh, the wondrous love of God that really makes all things new and that alone can do so.

Observe how the father blots out the past. He goes to meet the son as if nothing had ever happened, he embraces him and kisses him as if he had always been most dutiful and exemplary in all his conduct! And how quickly he commands the servants to strip off the rags and the tatters of the far country, and remove from his son every trace and vestige of his evil past. He wipes out the past by all those actions in a way that no one else could do. He alone could forgive really, he alone could wipe out what the boy had done against the family and against himself, and he did so. He strips off every trace of the past. That is always the first thing that happens when a sinner turns to God in the way we have been describing. We go to Him and expect just as little as the prodigal who had expected to be made a servant. How infinitely does God transcend our highest expectations when He begins to deal with us. All we ask for is a kind of new beginning. God amazes and surprises us in His very first action by blotting out our past. And that, after all, is what we desire most of all. How can we be happy and be free in view of our past? Even if we no longer do a certain action, or commit a particular sin, there is the past, there is what we have done already.

That is the problem. Who can deliver us from our past? Who can erase from the book of our life what we have done already? There is but One! And He can! The world tries to persuade me that it does not matter, that I can turn my back upon it and forget it. But I cannot forget it, it keeps on returning. And it makes me miserable and wretched. I try everything but still my past remains, a solid, awful, terrible fact. Can I never get free from it? Can I ever be rid of it? There is only One who can strip it off my back. I only know that my rags and tatters have really gone when I see them on the Person of Jesus Christ the Son of God, who wore them in my stead and became a curse in my place. The Father commanded Him to take my filthy rags off me and He has done so. He bore my iniquity, He clothed and covered Himself with my sin. He has taken it away and has drowned it in the sea of God's forgetfulness. And when I see and believe that God in Christ has not only forgiven but also forgotten my past, who am I to try to look for it and to find it? My only consolation when I consider the past is that God has blotted it out. No other could do so. But He has done so. It is the first essential step in a new beginning. The past must be erased, and in Christ and His atoning death, it is!

But in order to have a really new start, I require something further. It is not enough that every trace of my past be removed. I require something in the present. I desire to be clothed, I must be robed. I need confidence to start afresh and to face life and its people and its problems. Though the father met the boy and kissed him, that alone would not have given him confidence. He would have known that everyone was looking at the rags and at the mud. But the father does not stop at that. He clothes the boy with dress that is worthy of a son and places a ring on his finger. He gives him the status of a son and the external proofs of that station. He announces to all that his son has returned and so clothes him as to make him feel unashamed when he meets people. No one else could do that but the father. Others could have taken the boy in and have helped him. But no one could make him a son but the father, and give him his position and provide him with the wherewithal.

It is precisely the same with us when we turn to God. He not only forgives and blots out the past, He makes us sons. He gives us new life and new power. He will so assure you of His love that you will be able to face men unashamed. He will clothe you with the robe of Christ's righteousness. He will not only tell you that He regards you as a child, but make you feel that you are one. As you look at yourself you will not know yourself. You will look at your body and see this priceless robe, you will look at your feet and see them newly shod, you will look at your hand and see the ring and signet of God's love. And as you do so, you will feel that you can face the whole world without apology; yes, and face the Devil also, and all the powers that fooled you in the past and ruined your life. Without this standing and confidence a new start is a mere figment of the imagination. The world only tries to clean the old suit and make it look respectable. God in Christ alone can clothe us with the new robe and really make us strong. Let the world try to point its finger and remind us of our past. Let it do its worst, we have but to look at the robe and the shoes and the ring, and all is well.

And if you require a clear proof of the actuality of all this, it is to be found in the fact that even the world has to acknowledge that it is true. Listen to the servant speaking to the elder brother. What does he say? Is it, "A strange-looking man in rags and tatters has come from somewhere"? No! "Thy brother is come." How did he know he was the brother? He had seen the father's actions and had heard the father's words. He would never have recognized the son, but the father did, even while he was yet a long way off. The father knew! And God knows you. When you go to Him and allow Him to clothe you, everyone will get to know it. Even the elder brother knew it. It was the very last thing he wanted to know. But the conclusion to be drawn from the singing, and the noise of jubilation and happiness was unavoidable. He is too mean to say "my brother"; but he, even he, has to say "this thy son." I do not promise that all will like you and speak well of you if you give yourself to God in Christ. Many will certainly hate you and persecute you and try to laugh at you and do many things to you. But, in doing so, they will actually be testifying that they also have seen that you are a new man, that you have been made anew and have been given a new start.

What More Do You Require?

Here is an opportunity for a real new beginning. It is the only way. God Himself has made it possible by sending His only begotten Son into this world, to live and die and rise again. It matters not at all what you have been, nor what you are like at the moment. You have but to come to God confessing your sin against Him, casting yourself upon His mercy in Jesus Christ, acknowledging that He alone can save and keep. You will find that

> The past shall be forgotten,
> A present joy be given,
> A future grace be promised,
> A glorious crown in heaven.

Come! Amen.

NOTES

The Two Builders

Clovis Gillham Chappell (1882–1972) was one of American Methodism's best-known and most effective preachers. He pastored churches in Washington, D.C.; Dallas and Houston, Texas; Memphis, Tennessee; and Birmingham, Alabama; his pulpit ministry drew great crowds. He was especially known for his biographical sermons that made biblical figures live and speak to our modern day. He published about thirty volumes of sermons.

This message was taken from *The Sermon on the Mount*, published in New York in 1930 by Lamar and Whitmore.

Clovis Gillham Chappell

11

THE TWO BUILDERS

Matthew 7:24–27

THIS PARABLE MARKS the close of Matthew's version of the Sermon on the Mount. Jesus has been preaching to a vast and interested multitude. They have listened to Him with mingled amazement and gladness. In conclusion He tells them, as He tells us, that it is not enough to listen, even though we listen with reverent approval. It is not enough to listen, even though we listen with keen appreciation and with emotions deeply stirred. If our listening is to be of any worth, it must lead to action. We must not only hear, we must obey. It was to enforce this truth that Jesus told the story of the two builders whose buildings were tested by the storm.

All Who Hear Are Builders

The first fact that Jesus brings home to our hearts in this story is that all who hear are builders. Of course we build whether we hear or not; but it is to the hearers that He is confining Himself in this parable. There are the wise builders, and there are the foolish. Jesus, as we have noticed before, is constantly dividing folks into two groups. There are those who have the wedding garment, and those who do not. There are those who travel the broad way, and those who travel the narrow. There are those who are spiritually alive, and those who are spiritually dead. We of today do not relish such divisions. But the fact remains that Jesus makes them, and makes them constantly.

Now, the wise man is a builder. He is constructing something. He is building his own character. He is building his soul home. He is building the temple in

153

which he is to spend eternity. The same is equally true of the foolish man. He, too, is building. He, too, is constructing the temple or the hovel or the sty in which he is to spend eternity. Both alike are builders.

This is true of all of us. We are building all the time, whether wisely or foolishly. We are building by everything that we do. We are building by every thought that we think. We are building by every word that we speak, every dream that we dream, every picture that we hang upon the walls of our imagination, every ambition that we cherish. All these go to make up the material that enters into the structure that we are building for the ages.

Some of us are putting some shoddy stuff into our buildings. We are putting material that cannot stand the test of the storm. That oath that you swore, that thoughtless blasphemy that you flung from your lips, that was poor material. That foul story that you told, that unclean thing that you did, that, too, was shoddy. That time that you ran with the multitude to do evil out of sheer cowardice; that time when you remained silent when you should have spoken—that, too, was poor stuff to put into your soul temple. That time you clutched your money in the presence of a pressing need; that time you passed by on the other side when a wounded life was calling to you—that also was shoddy. The fact that you are standing today, though a member of the church, with your membership hidden away in the country or buried in your trunk, trying to play the neutral when God is needing soldiers—that means that you are putting some very flimsy stuff into your building.

Then some are building staunchly and beautifully. That was fine material that the widow put into her building when she threw in her two mites for love's sake. That was fine material that Daniel put into his soul palace when he purposed in his heart that he would not defile himself. That was rugged and substantial stuff that Joseph used when he fled his temptation, even though his escape cost him the horrors of a dungeon. That is fine material you are using as you walk life's common ways in loving loyalty to your duty as God gives you to see your duty.

But whether we are building wisely or foolishly, we are all building. Nor are our lives fragmentary things. They are not so much brick and lumber and mortar and nails flung down in confusion. Every life is a whole, with certain definite moral characteristics. For instance, when the Old Testament tells us that a certain king did evil in the sight of the Lord, that does not mean that every act of his life was necessarily wicked. It means only that the man was inwardly evil and that, therefore, the prevailing tone of his life was of the same character. Likewise, when it says of another that he did that which was right in the sight of the Lord, this does not mean that every act of his life was perfect, but that its prevailing tone, its moral characteristic, was upright and pure. But whether wisely or foolishly, we are all building.

The Buildings Are Going to Be Tested

The second fact that our Lord brings to our attention is this, that the buildings that we are constructing, the characters we are making, are going to be tested. For this reason we are not to build for fair weather only. We must build with a view to hours of crises. We must build with a view to times of tempest. For, sooner or later, to all the testing comes. Upon you, and you, and you some day the storm will surely break.

This is the case whether we build wisely or foolishly. The building of the foolish man is going to be tested, but the building of the wise man is going to be tested too. God does not coddle His saints. He does not protect them from the stress and strain of life. He never promises them exemption from conflict. Our Lord prays for us, but He never prays that we may dodge the storm and have an easy time. "I pray not that thou shouldest take them out of the world, but that thou shouldest keep them from the evil." He means for us not to flee the tempest, but to face it and defy it. For to all the storm must come.

We realize the fact of the coming storm in the making of our material structures. We do not want a garment that will spot and fade the moment a drop of water touches it. We seek to have those that will retain their shape and color. When I was a boy, seersucker suits were sometimes worn in summer. But woe to the man that was overtaken by a rain! By the time he got dry his sleeves were to his elbows and his trousers to his knees. The ship that is constructed to sail only upon a glassy sea and under blue skies will not do for oceans like ours, where the heavens so often become black and where the seas are so often whipped by the tempest. Our bridges must be able to sustain more than their own weight. They must stand heavy tests. They must be built with a view to a city's traffic. In the building of our houses, whether private or public, we must take the tempest into consideration. To fail to do so would mean disaster.

While I was pastor in Washington a few years ago there came a terrific snowstorm. For more than thirty-six hours the snow fell until it lay deep on the earth and upon the roofs of the houses. There was a theater in that city that was a thing of beauty, but the architect had only sunny days in his eye when he planned it. He foolishly built without due regard to the coming storm. Therefore, when the snow lay some thirty inches deep upon it, the strain was too great. The roof crashed, and more than one hundred lives were lost in the disaster.

Now, Christ tells us frankly that the test is coming to ourselves. Upon some here present heavy storms have already broken. You are in God's house even now having by His grace come bravely through more than one trying tempest. Others of you have seen your lives crash in ruins. For, while there are some who have storm-proof religion, there are others whose religion is a plaything of the winds. The rude fists of the tempest dash it ruthlessly aside. But to all the storm comes. Just when it is coming we do not know. It may be today; it may be tomorrow. Just how it is coming we do not know. It does not come to all alike.

1. Sometimes the storm breaks upon us in the guise of a great temptation. We are brought suddenly face to face with an inducement to evil that we feel, if we accept, must line our pathway with roses. If we refuse, life will become a desert. A successful young banker said to me the other day, very seriously and very earnestly: "The most persistent petition in my prayer is this: 'Lead us not into temptation.'" It is a wise prayer. We need to pray it, every one of us; for any hour our crisis may be upon us. Any hour we may be overwhelmed if He does not help us weather the gale.

2. The storm may come in the guise of some bitter personal loss. One day out of the blue the news may come that you have lost every penny that you possessed; that from plenty you have been reduced to poverty; that the wolf is now howling at your very door. Or, worse still, it may be some bitter personal loss— the slipping out of your home of a loved one dearer to you than life. It may mean the sundering of ties most tender and binding. I wonder, when the storm comes, if you will be able to say with the staunch faith of Job: "The Lord gave, and the Lord hath taken away: blessed be the name of the Lord."

Or, what is even harder to bear, if we read Job's record aright, there may come to you the complete loss of health. There may come the persistent gnawing of physical pain. Sentence of death may be passed upon you weary months before its execution. You may be called on to suffer and to suffer long. Torture may sit astride your chest and clutch at your throat and lay its burning hands so heavily upon your lips that at times you cannot pray. When that terrible storm comes, I wonder if you can stand up against it bravely enough to say: "Though he slay me, yet will I trust him."

3. Then the storm may be of a different character. Instead of blowing away your treasure, it may bring it in larger abundance. When the Israelites were in the wilderness, there came to them a time of storm. But it blew nothing away. It brought them wealth. They were half buried in delicious quails. But those days of luxury

158 / Classic Sermons on the Parables of Jesus

were by no means their best days. They became days
of pestilence and plague. These people could not en-
dure prosperity. The place of their enrichment became
a graveyard. The name of it signifies the "graves of
lust." They were made to realize the tragic fact that
there is a destruction that wasteth at noonday.

It is such a tempest that constitutes one of the chief
dangers of our land today. Our spiritual progress lags
so far behind our material progress. We are rich in
things, but often deadly poor in the wealth that outlasts
the ages. It is hard to face a tempest of adversity. It is
harder still to stand against an avalanche of prosperity. As the Roman girl who promised to lead an invad-
ing army into her city if each soldier would give her
the bracelet from his own arm was crushed under the
weight of her own wealth, so many a one is crushed
today. Happy is the man who lives in the consciousness of the fact that his life consists not in the abundance of the things that he possesses.

4. Finally, to every one of us is coming the test of the
judgment. This is true of those who build wisely. It is
true of those who build foolishly. Every one of us is on
the road to the hour of testing. That is as certain as the
fact of life. It is as certain as the fact of death. It is as
certain as the fact of God. "Every man must give an
account of himself to God. . . . For we must all stand
before the judgment seat of Christ. . . . For it is appointed
unto man once to die, but after this the judgment."

How supremely important, therefore, that we should
build wisely and well, for every man's building is going
to be tested!

> Build thee more stately mansions, O my soul,
> As the swift seasons roll.
> Leave thy low-vaulted past,
> Let each new temple, nobler than the last,
> Shut thee from heaven with a dome more vast,
> Till thou at length art free,
> Leaving thine outgrown shell by life's
>   unresting sea.

The Issues of the Testing
Are Not the Same for All

The final fact that our Lord brings before us is that the issues of the testing are not going to be the same for all.

1. Some are not going to be able to stand the test. This is true of all whose lives are not founded on Himself and His teaching. What a bold and daring declaration! Yet He makes it, and makes it without the slightest flinching. He makes it without the least modification. "If you do not build on me," He says frankly, "your house will not stand. One day the tempest will swoop down upon it and tear it to fragments. One day there will be a crash, then shreds of wreckage upon the raging waters, and the ruin will be complete." "For other foundation can no man lay than that is laid, which is Jesus Christ."

2. But there are those, thank God, that are going to pass through the testing without loss. There are those that are going to outride all storms. There are those that are going to weather all gales. This is true of all who have built their lives upon Jesus Christ. For such a life it is going to be written in time, and it is going to be written in eternity: "It fell not." "He shall be like a tree planted by rivers of water." He remains steadfast. He is unhurt amidst the crash of tempests and the wreck of worlds. "For the world passeth away, and the lust thereof; but he that doeth the will of God abideth forever." Such are the stupendous claims of Jesus, and these high claims have been vindicated countless millions of times. Lives built on Him really do stand the test.

A few years ago a mission worker who was a beautiful saint went to comfort a friend who had lost a wife. If this friend was a Christian at all, he was only nominally so. The minister spoke to him of the consolations of the Gospel. But the bereaved man turned on him bitterly and said: "Have you ever lost your wife?" The preacher answered in the negative. "Well," said the other impatiently, "you don't know what you are talking about. Wait until you have a sorrow like mine and see if your Christ can meet the test."

The preacher went away with a sense of failure. But the testing time was closer to him, too, than he dreamed. Suddenly, without the slightest warning, the news came that his brilliant and gifted wife had been killed in a railroad accident. The remains were brought to the city and taken to the mission hall. This grief-stricken husband stood by the coffin of his wife to speak. He said: "Some six months ago I tried to comfort a bereaved husband, but I failed. He said I did not know what I was talking about. Is he here?" And the man stood up. The preacher then continued: "My friend, I know today. I am in the midst of a sorrow like your sorrow, and I want to tell you that, while my heart is bleeding and broken, I find His grace sufficient. I find that His hand holds me and steadies me. I find that my skies are as bright as the promises of God, and that underneath are the Everlasting Arms." May you find your foundation so secure when you come to your testing! If you do, you must build upon the Rock of Ages.